BROTHERS OF HABIT

BROTHERS OF HABIT

Life in a Monastery

by

Lionel Marshall Walker

ROBERT HALE · LONDON

© *Lionel Marshall Walker 1981*
First published in Great Britain 1981

ISBN 0 7091 9144 8

Robert Hale Limited
Clerkenwell House
Clerkenwell Green
London EC1R 0HT

Photoset in Great Britain by
Rowland Phototypesetting Ltd, Bury St Edmunds, Suffolk
and printed by St Edmundsbury Press, Bury St Edmunds, Suffolk
Bound by Weatherby Woolnough Ltd

Contents

To my wife,
in appreciation of her encouragement
and help in the writing of this book

1

Setting the Stage

This book has been written to try to explain to the interested inquirer the reasons that prompt men and women to leave their normal everyday life and enter a religious order. It also explains their reasons for leaving, if or when, they reach their breaking point.

As far as I am aware, there is no literature available from which those living outside can get any idea of the daily life within a monastery. Although many novels and television and cinema shows and plays, have been written which depict the subject, these tend to confuse rather than instruct, since they are produced for entertainment and are therefore not necessarily authentic.

Certainly, when I entered a monastery, I found that many of my preconceived ideas were inaccurate. Many strange ideas exist as to what goes on behind the walls of a religious institution. (Incidentally, the walls are there to keep the 'world' out, and not to keep the inhabitants in.) Many opinions are based upon publications on the subject, written by scandalized Victorians anxious to defend the 'virtue' of the Anglican Church against the then hated 'Romanists'. I was rather amused when an acquaintance of mine described the monasteries as "hotbeds of homosexuality". All I can say, in all honesty, is that homosexuals do sometimes find themselves in a monastery, as they do in other walks of life. Generally speaking, these unfortunate people, being of a religious nature, manage to behave at least as well as most heterosexuals under their vows of celibacy.

At this point, it would be well to enumerate the vows under which members of religious orders live. These vows are usually threefold: poverty, chastity and obedience. In the case of the Benedictine order, with which I am most familiar, St Benedict included in his Rule the additional instruction, *"Promittat de stabilitate sua et conversatione morum suorum et obedientiam"*, which is generally translated as "He shall promise stability, conversion of his life, and obedience". The purpose of completely renouncing one's will in this way, is so that one may have more time for prayer and meditation and so fuse oneself with God.

People generally find it hard to accept the presence of monasteries within the Anglican Church. There is, in fact, no reason why they should not exist as the Anglican Church is, and always has been, Catholic. Henry VIII, at the Reformation, did not deviate from the Catholic faith, only from the control of the Pope. The various wedges of dissension have been driven in since the Reformation. The bitterness, which existed between the two churches and which has now subsided, was only caused by religious bigotry on both sides.

There are many false ideas prevailing about religious houses concerning such things as the food allowance and the living conditions generally. For example, one entrant to the monastery said that he had expected never to see the outside world again once the big doors had closed behind him. This is far from the truth, as he found out, although he had entered a so-called 'enclosed' order. There are occasional exceptions to this in convents where the 'grills' system is still in operation and the nuns never leave the area enclosed by their grill. However, this system is rapidly dying out.

Again, some people are surprised to find that many monks receive a ration of tobacco and that a moderate amount of alcohol is allowed with meals on feast days. On the other hand, the furnishings of a monk's cell are usually austere by modern standards.

Having made the above brief remarks to 'set the stage', I intend to tell my story by describing various members of a typical community which is fictional and non-specific. Each man will have a chapter devoted to him under the name with which he started his life in religion. He is known as "Brother X" when clothed as a novice, and "Dom X", in the Benedictine order, when he becomes 'life professed'. I shall also add a brief account of the man's life prior to his entry into the monastery.

It is interesting to note that only about one man in ten attains life profession, the others reaching their breaking point before then, and leaving. It should also be noted that life profession is not absolutely binding today. There is still a method of leaving allowed by the Church, which is an honourable way if the correct procedure is followed.

I must make it clear that the characters in my book are fictitious and bear no relationship to any individual, living or dead. Each character will be quite unrecognizable as any one person, although each may have the characteristics of several people combined in him. There is no intention to characterize one particular person and if anyone imagines he sees his own personality portrayed in a character this is purely coincidental. Any name, religious or secular, which is used was picked at random and although some persons may bear the same religious name, this is again coincidental owing to the very limited number of names used in religious houses.

The actions of the characters are also fictitious. The only resemblance which they bear to fact is that the situation, as seen by the author, is one which might possibly arise within a monastery under the conditions described.

If the reader wishes to imagine the locality of the monastery in which the action takes place, he may assume that it is situated near the south coast of England.

I have tried not to dwell too much on the religious aspect of the monastic life and hope that this will not give the incorrect impression that this is neglected in religious houses. It is hoped that members of the Faith will forgive this deference to non-religious readers.

2

A Postulant, an Oblate and a Lay Brother

JOHN WILLIAM GATES

The reason why John William Gates is not called 'Brother' will be obvious after reading his case history.

His father was a successful grocer with a chain of six shops in Hull and the family were proud of their High Church connections. As we meet him, John, aged eighteen, has just left his grammar school and is under pressure to join the family business. His older brother is already managing one of his father's shops, his sister is married and living away from Hull and his younger brother is still at school.

The prospect of becoming a grocer was not at all to John's liking and he had other ideas. He was first introduced to the possibility of monastic life by a talk at the Men's Society of his church on P. F. Anson's book *The Call of the Cloister*. He was very intrigued with the idea and if the truth be told, he probably saw in it an escape from being pressed into the family business. After turning the matter over in his mind, John decided to go for a retreat in our monastery and his parents were pleased to see him taking this interest.

Arriving at the monastery, John immediately stated that he wished to join the community and was surprised when he was not received with open arms. The Church needs to be sure that the applicant has a vocation and is not entering for some less worthy motive.

Several visits later, having passed the scrutiny of the monastery officials, it only remained to reconcile his family to the idea. Naturally, they were disappointed that he was not going into the family business, but they gave him their blessing as they were pleased to give a son to the Church.

All hurdles overcome, John presented himself at the monastery on a bright morning in March, having travelled down from Hull the previous day. Spending the night at the Bonnington Hotel in Southampton Row, he had taken in a show at the Windmill Theatre as a 'final fling'.

The following morning he caught the train from the London terminal to the nearest station to the monastery, where he was picked up by the monastery car. He was taken into the guest reception by the monk on door duty and was collected by the novice master rather more quickly than he had hoped, before he had time to satisfy his curiosity regarding the shop, which sold books, crucifixes, rosaries and handicrafts, by means of which the monks sought to augment their finances.

The novice master greeted him affably, shaking hands and enquiring about his journey down. John admitted that he had stayed the night in London but omitted any reference to the Windmill Theatre, as he thought that this might be 'taboo'. The novice master then took him into the monastic enclosure for the first time, taking him to the cell accommodation on the upper floors via the rear stairway and telling him that he would not be allowed to use the main stairway until he joined the senior common-room in his last year in temporary vows. This rather shook John as the rear stairway was uncarpeted boards. True, these, stained and treated with linseed oil, shone like a newly oiled cricket bat, but the rest of the decorations were in desperate need of renewal. This was shortly to be done as the monks worked through the monastery. As John followed the novice master, dragging his suitcase behind him, he could not help comparing this with home.

The novice master deposited him in his new cell and left him to unpack and change into the shorts and cassock worn by all postulants. The door closed without a sound and John was left standing on a floor, stained dark oak, and polished with linseed oil and wax, the smell of which, along with an odour of incense, permeated the air. He was astounded to find a central-heating radiator which was hot to his hand but noted the meagre furnishings: a 'wardrobe' or rather an alcove with a curtain over it; a prie-dieu, in front of a hanging crucifix, which he tried and found the bare-board kneeler abominably hard to his unaccustomed knees; an empty bookcase for his books and a desk with a clean new blotter and writing materials and a hard chair. His gaze then fell upon the hospital-type bed which was harder than his own bed. On the whole the room depressed him, it seemed like a prison cell in comparison with his room at home.

He went to the window; it had a sill about a foot wide and shutters but no curtains. There was a glorious view of the extensive monastery grounds and he could see five or six figures, clothed in brown boiler suits, working in the vegetable garden. He thought that these must be the gardeners—little did he know that he would shortly be working with them.

He recovered from his day-dream with a start and realized that ten of the twenty minutes before the novice master returned had gone. He undid his case hastily and taking off his suit, he put on his shorts and cassock, in which he felt foolish and very conscious of the draught round his knees.

At that moment the novice master returned, knocking on the cell door before entry and explaining that cells were not lockable, but it was customary to knock before entering another's cell.

John was shown the bathroom and w.c. which he would use and then taken on a tour of the monastery. He was introduced to the infirmarian who would attend to him if he were sick, and the petty cash bursar, to whom he handed his money and from whom he would draw money if he had to go out of the monastery. He was also shown where to get fresh linen and underclothes, and where to place his dirty washing.

They then toured the ground floor where there were kitchens, sculleries and the refectory where the community ate. Next came the *statio* where the community assembled for offices. Entering the Lady Chapel, the postulant was dazzled by the magnificence of the gold altar and the statue of Our Lady with the infant Jesus. From here they went into the chapel and John was shown where to genuflect as he entered and where he would sit in the gallery, until he was given a place in choir.

At this point, the novice master consulted his watch and said he had a finance meeting, so he would find John a job to do and collect him when he was free. They then proceeded to the rear of the premises where the 'wayfarers' or tramps are fed and succoured. They are given a good meal and a bath, if desired, with plenty of soap and hot water. There was no dormitory but a comfortable day-room from which they were sent to a Salvation Army Hostel at night.

John was introduced as assistant to the kitchen staff and the novice master found him a bath to clean out. It was in a shocking state, as usual. The water, which had been left in, was black and sooty and when the novice master pulled the plug out a black slime was left from the waterline down.

Our postulant took one look and said, "Oh no! Not for me! I am off home!" He turned round and fled and, collecting his things from his cell, he set out to walk to the railway station over two miles away. If he had waited, he could have had a meal before he left and transport to the station. His was the quickest exit on record—two hours flat.

Postulants often provide a little light entertainment of this kind. One such arrived unannounced and said that he had come to be a monk. When interviewed, it was clear that he was neurotic and unsuitable. On being told this, he became agitated and said he had given up his lodgings and his job to join us. He was told that this was most unwise and that the correct procedure was to write for an interview and then stay with us for a few days so that we could get to know one another. We also like postulants to take six months' leave of absence from their job, so that they have not burnt their boats. Our friend was told that he could remain in the guest-house until he could find a job and lodgings, in which task we would assist him.

He made a nuisance of himself, going round the monks, telling them that the abbot was turning him out and quoting repeatedly John vi. 37, "The Lord Jesus Christ said; Him that cometh unto me I will in no wise cast out". He created such a disturbance that the abbot eventually had to call the police to have him put out.

Another case was that of a weedy-looking eighteen-year-old who arrived with his mother in a chauffeur-driven Daimler. The mother took charge of the situation from the start. She had brought her son to the monastery, as he was in poor health, and she thought the monastery was just the place for him, where he would have nothing to do but chant the choir office. The good lady was most upset when she was informed that he would have to undergo a medical examination at least as rigorous as that for the Army, since the monastic life would tax the strongest physique.

Another man came to us about whom we had reservations from the start, but he was allowed to try his vocation and enter as a postulant. After a couple of months, it was obvious that he was unsuitable, and, when told this, he said he was sorry as it was the best job that he had ever had.

Another applicant got as far as being clothed as a novice, but after several weeks it became clear that he had not got a vocation. When informed of this, he immediately went up to his cell and broke all the windows before departing.

As one of the brethren once remarked, "They come and they go—mostly they go."

BROTHER GEORGE

George Frederick Willington was a pharmacist and his dearest wish was to have a son to follow him in the pharmacy, which had been founded by his own father. As a young man, he had married a woman who was in a very delicate state of health, but who, rather late in life, presented him with the son that they had both longed for. The wife had a very bad time during the birth and she very nearly died. The boy struggled for survival and was reared with difficulty. There was no question of a second child, as the gynaecologist warned them that it was doubtful if the wife would survive another birth.

In due course the boy was sent away to boarding-school but at the age of thirteen years he developed an infection of the mastoid, which in those days, before the advent of antibiotics, necessitated surgery. This was a messy and sometimes dangerous operation and although the boy survived the surgery, in his low post-operative state, he developed pneumonia to which he succumbed.

His parents were heartbroken. The health of the wife, never very good, suffered greatly as a result of the bereavement and George sold his pharmacy and retired early to look after her. Fortunately they had enough money to do this.

George had made a regular annual retreat to our monastery, his wife going to a nearby convent, so he knew the monastery well. When his wife died a year or so after they had lost the boy, George was left without a relative in the world and, as is always the case in adversity, his religion came to his aid. His first thought was to retire into the monastery for a few weeks in order to sort himself out. He had become an extern oblate, so there was no problem over his entering.

It was clear to George that he had an affinity with the monastery, but he did not wish to commit himself fully to the life of a monk, even in the unlikely event of this being possible at his age. There were therefore two alternatives. Either he could become an intern oblate, whereby there would be no change in his status except that he would live in the monastery, or he could become a claustral oblate.

As an intern oblate he would assist with such work as gardening or clerical duties in exchange for his keep. He would provide his own habit and be at liberty to furnish his own cell, with the agreement of the abbot, and would be free within reason to leave the monastery for holidays. He would not have a monk's stall in choir, but would sit with the other oblates behind the choir. Otherwise he would take part in all the activities and ceremonies of the monastery.

As a claustral oblate, he would give up his income from

property and investments to the monastery, as in the case of a monk, but he would retain the capital and investments in his own name. He would not be free to leave for a holiday at will, but would be sent out on an annual 'rest' like the monks. He would be directed by the workmaster to perform any work of which he was capable.

Thus the oblates in a monastery hold a unique position. They wear the same habit as the novice, except that it does not have a hood. All oblates in the monastery are junior to the monks, but the monks serve them as a mark of humility. Men become oblates either when they are too old to become a monk, or when there are family dependents who might call on them at a later date, in which case the Church will not permit them to bind themselves irrevocably.

Our friend decided to become an intern oblate. It was not necessary for him to go through the ceremony of reception as an oblate, but only for him to receive the required two-thirds vote of the chapter to enable him to live in. In this case this went without question.

At the ceremony of receiving an oblate, the oblate master stands on the altar steps and the candidate kneels before him. The candidate then makes a formal declaration before the assembled oblates that he will henceforth order his life in accordance with the spirit of the Rule of St Benedict, under the guidance of the abbot and superiors of the monastery. Thus he makes his solemn promise to live in the spirit of the vows of poverty, chastity and obedience and the reformation of his life. The vow of poverty for the oblate is fulfilled by the donation of ten per cent of his income to charity. The vow of chastity is met by his undertaking to live a chaste life either in marriage or in the single state, whichever is appropriate to his circumstances. The vow of obedience is fulfilled by his undertaking to live under the direction of the oblate master and to make an annual retreat in the monastery.

The oblate who does not live in is presented with a token scapular which he wears under his shirt. This consists of two four-inch squares of black material, one worn on the back and one on the chest, which are joined together by black tapes to keep them in position. He is also presented with a Benedictine medallion which he wears on a silver chain around his neck. After a prayer that the new oblate will remain faithful to his promises, he then returns to the assembly of oblates who welcome him.

The life oblation takes place three years after the novice oblation. The ceremony is much the same except that the promises are made for life.

In the above, I am referring particularly to the Benedictine order but other orders generally have a similar oblate procedure.

In cases where the monastery is unsure whether a man should be admitted as an oblate living in the monastery or as a postulant contemplating full admittance as a monk, the case can be referred to the Council of Religious, who will advise and direct. There is no such problem if anyone wishes to become an extern oblate, provided that he is of good character and his local priest is willing to give him a reference.

BROTHER DOMINIC

James William Bowley started his working life at the age of fourteen years. He never had the privilege of an education, except that provided by the State and known as "elementary" when he was a boy. He was a bright lad with an intelligence which would have taken him a long way, given the opportunity. His favourite subjects were wood-work and metalwork.

James was the son of a London docker and was proud to be a genuine cockney, born within the sound of Bow Bells. His family moved to Liverpool just prior to the Depression of the 'thirties as his father had been offered a better job in the Liverpool docks. Our Brother Dominic also started work at the docks, which was the best opening that offered itself.

Then came the General Strike, followed by the Depression. The father lost his job but James, who was doing a man's job at a boy's rate of pay, still had a job and became the family bread-winner. His sister helped as she could always get a job—women could at that time but they were always paid less. The mother went out cleaning offices and she also took in washing. They managed somehow.

The father was desperate. He had heard that there was work back at the London docks so he left the family in Liverpool and hitch-hiked back to London. There, the docks were on strike, and the only jobs offered were to break the strike. He was sorely tempted but, being a union man, he knew that the union would see that he never worked again if he took the job.

After several abortive attempts to find work he returned to Liverpool, arriving soaked to the skin as he had walked much of the way in torrential rain. His constitution weakened by food shortage, he developed pneumonia and because there were no antibiotics in those days he did not survive the dreaded crisis.

Through all these troubles, James held on to his Anglo-Catholic faith and he made a retreat at our monastery whenever he could raise the fare. He determined to offer himself as a monk as soon as his family could manage without his pay packet.

When James was eighteen, he was sacked as he could now command a man's rate of pay. The mother and sister were still working and James tramped for miles trying to find work, but was unlucky.

Fate had not finished with James yet. His mother became very ill and had to be admitted to hospital. One of the young nurses at the hospital was especially kind to the family. After fighting a losing battle over four or five weeks, the mother, worn out before her time, slipped peacefully away. The nurse, whom they regarded as a personal friend, attended the funeral. She knew that James and his sister needed the money and asked if she could change her lodgings and live with them.

The two womenfolk could manage to run the home between them now and James determined to become a monk. When he broke the news to them they were both stunned for his sister had secretly hoped that he would marry the nurse. They both pleaded with him, but he was adamant. He wrote to the monastery immediately, and, after an interview, he was accepted for the lay brotherhood as a postulant. James had found his true vocation. He was not prepared for the snags but he faced them as they arose. He was ready to do the menial tasks as he said that he preferred the lay brotherhood and accepted that he could not become a choir monk and priest because he had not received the necessary education. This is a different attitude from that which one sometimes finds today amongst the lay brethren.

The workmaster soon realized that he had found a gem and Brother Dominic was put in charge of maintenance. He had entered into life vows as surely as the sun sets. Never was the place so well maintained. There was no need to report blown bulbs for they were spotted and replaced, as were dripping tap washers, and radiators that needed bleeding.

He was given a free hand in the refitting of the workshops and he acquired a metal lathe, through the widow of a deceased oblate, which was his pride and joy. With it he was able to do many jobs which previously had had to be paid for. He started the manufacture of crucifixes making the wooden crosses himself and buying in the figure. The finished product was perfect.

Not only was his work commendable, but also his observance was an example to all. Given the necessary education he would have made an excellent priest. As a lay brother, he was not bound to the full choir office, but he always insisted on saying it. The father in charge of lay brethren stopped him from saying the night office privately, as he was straining himself unduly in trying to do this as well as his work as a lay brother.

Brother Dominic was never robust, probably due to his early privations, although he was physically strong. On one occasion, when he was in bed with influenza, the community physician examined him and his heart condition gave cause for concern. He was in his early sixties then and the doctor prescribed less energetic work. He protested, but the doctor was adamant; there was a systolic murmur and this required attention. He would like Brother Dominic to see a specialist.

The specialist said there was some valvular damage and

he must do less strenuous work. More help was provided in the workshop and the abbot charged him to act only in an advisory capacity. He must not climb the stairs, but must use the goods lift, forbidden to the fit. He must stay in bed until 7.00 a.m. instead of rising at 5.00 a.m. with the others and he must take a rest at midday, lying on his bed for two hours. These instructions irked him, but he was too good a monk to disobey.

This went on for over two years until the doctor reported a deterioration and Brother Dominic was removed to hospital for observation. The surgeons wanted to operate, saying that this would make life easier and would prolong it. He now had to sleep propped up on pillows.

Brother Dominic wanted to know his chances if he refused surgery and was told that he might last another five years or he might die that night. Brother Dominic said that applied to all of us, and asked the abbot's permission to refuse surgery. Permission was granted and he was discharged without the operation being carried out.

As time passed he became increasingly unable to help himself but thanks to the devoted attention of the infirmarian and his staff, he passed his seventieth birthday. He said he was ready to go when God called him but as it turned out he lasted two more years, passing away peacefully just short of his seventy-third year.

The community mourned him. To juniors he was their 'living rule'; to seniors he was the lay brother who outshone many a choir monk in observance and discipline.

His sister and the nurse, both of them still unmarried and getting on in years, attended his funeral. With the advent of a realistic retirement pension their needs were provided for in their retirement.

There was one amusing incident concerning Brother Dominic which is worth recording. He possessed a trait peculiar in the British working man, in that he hated the use of bad language, even when totally frustrated. The nearest that he ever came to it was when he was awaiting the arrival of a supply of figures for his beloved crucifixes. There was one size, very popular in the shop, which we had run out of several weeks before. Brother Dominic had made and polished a supply of crosses in readiness. He always used wax polish to treat the crosses. It was more laborious to use than french polish, but it brought out the grain and produced a richer finish than the easier method.

At last, the long-awaited consignment arrived. Brother Dominic was unpacking them and it was plain that he was getting more and more exasperated as he searched the packing material. On being asked what was the matter, he answered, "The figures have arrived, but the packer has forgotten to send the special nails. After all these weeks, no nails. Can't finish the job still." He was very red in the face and burst out, "I hope the blooming packer has constipation for a week!"

3

Murder in the Monastery

The title of this chapter sounds rather like that of a 'whodunnit' but, in fact, it is a statement of stark reality. Fortunately, it did not take place in our monastery.

Monks live a very unnatural existence and explosive situations develop for a monk cannot relieve tension by visiting the cinema or pub. For this reason, monks are given a 'rest' outside the monastery each year, going either to relatives, a quiet guest-house, or another monastery. Monastic hospitality is reciprocal, thus monks get a complete change at the cost only of their travelling expenses and can even get abroad very cheaply.

A member of our community spent his 'rest' at a German monastery. On arrival, he was given a vacant cell and was expected to live and eat with the host community, taking a packed lunch and going walking during the day, saying his monastic office as he went. A monk is always bound to say his office, unless dispensed for illness.

Often oblates of the host monastery will entertain a visiting monk. Once, one of our monks was on a lecture tour in America and on completion of the tour he was invited to spend his 'rest' at the home of an oblate. His hosts wanted to take him into the Rocky Mountains and explained that it would entail a 5.30 a.m. start as it was a very long car journey. "Not to worry," said our monk to his hostess, "I am used to rising at five o'clock, I will rise myself and knock you up." There was a deathly silence. Later his host told him that he must never use this expression in America. Innocuous enough in England, in America it meant that he was offering to put the lady in the family way.

Returning to our friend in Germany, he had been entertained by the oblates and one day had been out walking on his own. On his return to the monastery, he was surprised to find a patrol car belonging to the German police parked outside and two burly policemen guarding the door. They challenged him and immediately whisked him off to a private room, where two police officers in plain clothes sat behind a table. They wanted to know where he had been all day and if he knew two of the German community. He admitted that he did, and asked what it was all about, but was dismissed without being told.

When he reached his room, a messenger from the abbot immediately appeared. Would he go to the office? On entering the abbot's office, our monk was informed what had happened. It appeared that two of the monks had never agreed. They worked together in the kitchens, but the abbot told them that they must live in harmony, and he had refused to separate them. All had gone well for several weeks, when our monk arrived and they had packed his food for the day he went out alone. But later in the morning there had been another altercation. One monk had been carrying a rolling-pin in his hand because he was rolling pastry and he had hit his brother monk on the head with it. This monk had staggered back and fallen, hitting his head on the corner of the table and then lying still. He was found to be dead when examined by the monastery doctor.

The police were called and the monk who had struck the blow was charged with murder. I do not believe he intended to kill; he had a violent temper and had struck out in blind rage, unfortunately, the recipient of the blow had struck his head in his fall. Nevertheless, the striker was culpable for he had not heeded the abbot's warning and tried to keep himself under control. The result was the death of a brother monk.

At the trial which followed, his counsel made out as good a case as possible for accidental death. Nevertheless the monk was found guilty and executed for this was before the death penalty was abolished in Germany.

The atmosphere in the monastery was one of shocked disbelief. The media spread the incident all over the headlines of Europe and the general public lapped it up. As the abbot remarked, "If a man runs away with his secretary, it is not news. If an abbot runs off with his secretary, it is splashed across all the headlines." Everybody knew what the abbot meant, but they had to smile, since the abbot's secretary was an aged and ponderous monk.

It is a salutary thought that if the condemned man had not been a monk, he would conceivably have been dealt with less severely. As it was he had been treated with the utmost rigour of the law.

Truly, from those who receive much, is much expected.

4

Ian Michael Macdonald

Ian Michael Macdonald was another postulant who never reached the novitiate. He was the son of an Aberdeen doctor and a member of the Scottish Episcopal Church which is closely allied with the Anglo-Catholic Church. He had first encountered the monastic life during a visit to the Loire Valley in France.

At the age of nineteen, despite the disapproval of his father, he decided to abandon university entrance and become a monk. He sought an interview with our novice master who tried to persuade him to complete his university course first. The next day he saw the abbot who also tried to dissuade him and sent him home for three months to reconsider.

Exactly three months later, the boy applied again. The abbot thought that it would do no harm to let him enter as a postulant as if there was no vocation, he would quickly leave. He was therefore examined by the community doctor and passed as fit.

At home, his mother, knowing his volatile temperament, made him promise to send a letter, mentioning a distant relative, if things did not work out and she would send a telegram saying that his father was ill and asking him to return home immediately. The good lady thought that the monastery was out to trap her son into staying. In fact the opposite is the case—it is much easier to leave than it is to enter, until one decides to take life vows.

Ian duly presented himself, was attired in cassock and shorts and taken on the usual tour of the monastery. After his first meal in the lowest place in the refectory, he was

27

given his first lesson on how to conduct himself in the monastery. He was junior to all and must rise when his senior entered the room. He should at all times keep his hands out of sight, except when working or holding his office book. He must not whistle or sing unless singing the office. He must always keep his eyes down and not watch others. This is called "custody of the eyes" and is an aid to 'recollection', or keeping the mind trained on God. He should never speak to a senior unless spoken to. He must not speak during the Greater Silence, (from about 9.00 p.m. until after breakfast the following day). He must restrict speech to the minimum at other times, except at recreation, when he would be encouraged to converse on any subject except politics or sex. He must always be clothed in the correct attire. In the corridors walking to the bathroom, a dressing-gown or his cassock should be worn. He must never go with a towel round his waist. He must wear a brown boiler suit when doing work for which a cassock is not suitable.

With that, he was dismissed and told that more instructions would follow later. Any deviations from the above must be confessed before the novitiate at the weekly chapter of faults, since they are faults, not sins, which must be confessed regularly in the confessional.

The chapter of faults is a chapter at which faults are confessed in public, starting with the abbot and working downwards. There is a separate chapter for novices.

He was next introduced to his confessor whom he would see weekly, and to the storekeepers. The infirmarian supplies medicines on demand and looks after the sick on instructions from the doctor. He investigates all who do not respond to the rising bell. The second storekeeper supplies all clothing replacements and the third keeps toilet requirements, razor blades, toothpaste and so on. To visit any of the storekeepers is the only time that a junior is permitted in the senior cell corridor.

After this, the novice master took charge of his personal possessions, which would be kept until life profession. One's watch is always handed back, since the only clock is the master clock usually kept in the *statio*, where the community assembles. This, incidentally, is the official monastery time, irrespective of whether it is fast or slow by G.M.T. One always sets one's watch by it.

The novice master then checked through the official list of clothing and books which one is allowed to bring in. At this stage any surplus is taken away and any deficiency is made up from the stores.

By then, it was nearly time for the afternoon office of vespers and Ian was conducted into the gallery where newcomers and sick brethren sit, overlooking the community. After vespers he was instructed to find his own way in to tea, as this, like breakfast, is not a main meal and one does not process in.

Ian walked into the refectory and stood awaiting grace as before. He was signalled by the next postulant, to say his own grace, and collect his own tea from the trolley, where there was a tea urn, sugar and milk. There were baskets of cut bread and bowls of butter and jam on the table. He was impressed by the complete silence in which the meal was partaken.

When he had finished, there was a tap on his shoulder and the novice master stood behind him. He explained to Ian that it was now study time. He was sent to his cell to await being called.

After about twenty minutes in his cell, there was a tap on his door and a novice entered and said, "Your turn with the novice master," and vanished.

Ian went as instructed and knocked and entered. The novice master was writing and Ian stood for some minutes before being invited to sit. (First lesson absorbed.) The cell was a facsimile of his own, but there were two extra chairs and it was lined with bookshelves.

Ian was first questioned regarding the Rule and then about his attainments in Latin and Greek at school. The novice master selected a Latin book, opened it and requested Ian to translate. Ian stumbled through half a page. The novice master said there were three Latin textbooks, and Ian would start at book two. This appeared like a conjurer's rabbit, along with a notebook. Ian would be summoned each study period to report on his progress. He was told to go to his gallery-seat for meditation and then follow the procession in to dinner.

He tried to meditate, but his mind wandered onto the events of the day. He must ask for advice about this. His back ached from kneeling so long, but at last the bell tolled and he went in to dinner.

The community stood until the abbot entered. A reader at the lectern then read from the Rule and a portion of scripture. On completion, the door opened, all sat, and a trolley came in with soup plates and a large pan of hot soup.

The guests were served first, then the community, starting with the abbot and working down. Ian's stomach was rumbling and he fervently hoped that this was not audible, and the soup would last out.

The reader was now reading aloud the book of the day, concerning the potato famine in Ireland. The novice beside Ian righted Ian's cup and filled it with water and then offered him bread. The soup arrived at last. It was unseasoned, and the condiments had vanished up the table. It appeared that seniors must have these first.

Ian realized that the top table had now been cleared of soup and that the trolley had arrived with the main course. Two aluminium bowls of vegetables were laid on the visitor's table, two before the abbot and two before the senior lay brother.

At last Ian's plate arrived and he wondered what the food was. A hard-boiled egg floated in an unidentifiable savoury mix but, with the vegetables, it tasted good enough.

Without warning, a large enamel kettle was thrust over his shoulder and his remaining half cup of water was filled with cocoa. He soon learnt to empty his water before the cocoa arrived, unless, as some did, he wished to dilute the strong cocoa. He looked round for a pudding, but St Benedict only prescribed two courses "so that he who cannot eat the one, shall make his meal of the other".

Suddenly, the abbot rang a little bell. The reader stopped in mid-sentence, and said in Latin what Ian thought started "May the Lord have mercy. . . ." It was a request for the abbot's blessing. The community immediately stood and filed out in order after the abbot, bowing to the crucifix over the abbot's chair. The abbot had said a short grace in Latin before leaving.

The novice master met Ian and conducted him to the junior common-room, where the rest of the novitiate stood awaiting them. Ian was introduced, and he wondered why some novices wore a short scapular whilst others wore a long one. This was because some were in temporary vows, when they spend the first two of three years in the novitiate. The scapular is the length of material hanging from the shoulders, to which the hood is attached.

The novice master gave them permission to smoke and explained that they were allowed twenty cigarettes or one ounce of tobacco weekly. This was necessary owing to the widespread addiction to tobacco but non-smoking entrants were not allowed to start.

Conversation ranged over a wide field, finally resting on homes and families for Ian's benefit.

The bell rang for compline and the Major Silence. Ian had been told to arise next morning at 7.30 a.m. and he thought this was reasonable. The rude awakening came later.

After compline Ian went to bed but he lay awake for a long time, before falling into a fitful sleep. He awoke to the clanging of the rising bell and then realized that it was only 5.00 a.m. At 7.15 he dressed and went to breakfast. The familiar urns were there and he took coffee and went to his place. The friendly novice led him into the kitchen where, in one big oven there were piles of plates separated by aluminium rings and covers. The novice handed Ian an oven cloth, and Ian helped himself. The plate contained one large rasher of bacon only—no egg, sausage, or kidney. Ian soon learnt that one gets either bacon, or egg, or sausage, or kidney in a monastery—never all four together.

On the table there were the usual baskets of cut bread with butter and marmalade. Ian soon learnt the art of keeping his eyes down and yet seeing what was happening. Monks communicated by signs. The flat hand over a cup was a refusal, a chopping sign with the edge of the hand on the other palm meant, "Give me half, please", the same sign pointing at another monk meant, "Will you share this with me?" There were many such signs.

The big bell tolled. Ian added his dirty crockery to the rest on the trolley and hurried to his seat for prime, after which the novice master met him and reminded him that he had forgotten to genuflect to the altar before leaving. Arriving at Ian's cell, he reminded him that his bed must be made before breakfast. Ian coloured up and retorted that he had not been told the latter but the novice master remarked quietly that Ian must learn to accept criticism without comment. There would be a long list of faults in his early days, as is expected.

After this explanation, Ian was somewhat mollified. The novice master suggested that he write home during the afternoon siesta. He would be allowed one letter per week, which must be tendered unsealed to the novice master, who would likewise open incoming letters. This again stung Ian, but it was explained that this right of censorship was usually only a token one.

The bell for conventual Mass tolled. After Mass, Ian, dressed in his gumboots and brown boiler suit, reported to the workmaster who put him in the hands of another monk who conducted him to the main vehicle entrance of the monastery, where a concrete surface was being laid. A concrete-mixing lorry was backing up, and Ian was given a shovel and told to shovel concrete.

Ian was as fit as most, but he fell behind the others who helped him with his stint. He was splashed from head to foot with concrete, and was unable to keep pace with the second load. The last straw was when his boot became full of concrete. His temper overcame him and, throwing down his shovel, he stamped off back to the novice master, before the others knew where he was going.

The novice master, who was writing, looked surprised as Ian burst in and enquired quietly, "Whatever is the matter?" Ian poured forth his complaint. The novice master stopped him and quietly told him to take a shower and change into his cassock and then he would be heard. The two looked one another straight in the eyes, then Ian turned to comply with the request.

On Ian's return, the novice master greeted him kindly and asked him to state his complaint. He then explained that there were different reactions from postulants, first introduced to manual labour. This job was not beyond Ian's physical capacity for he had been passed as fit. He had been given a difficult task to test his vocation. A quiet explanation to the monk in charge would have produced help.

The superior then pointed out where Ian was at fault. He had lost his temper, entered the house in filthy gumboots, leaving a trail of wet cement behind him and failed to approach his senior according to the Rule. These flaws must be overcome if he intended to reach life profession. He must now make amends for his faults by humbly performing the penance of cleaning up the mess that he had made, using a mop and bucket. Also his gumboots must be washed before the concrete dried on them.

These statements were made gently and quietly, but nevertheless with a ring of authority, so that Ian felt ashamed of his outburst. He retired, thinking that he would never make life profession. He cleaned up as he had been bidden, and then went in to lunch, to which he did not do credit.

After the meal, he retired to his cell for the siesta. He made up his mind and wrote to his mother as arranged. As it happened, his letter left immediately. The next two days Ian endured in a daze.

In the evening, the novice master brought Ian a telegram, showing great concern, and said Ian must be on the night train. He would take him to the station himself and make sure he caught the midnight train from London. Ian protested that the next morning would do, as he did not relish the thought of the uncomfortable overnight journey, but the senior would have none of it. He said Ian must go immediately and gave him some sandwiches as he would miss his dinner. Ian was told to dress in suit and overcoat and they would leave in fifteen minutes.

When a letter arrived later, telling the monastery to

keep Ian's effects which he had left behind and explaining the situation, the novice master remarked to the abbot that the foolish boy could have left in comfort on any train of his choice if he had not been deceitful.

It is a fact that any member of the community can leave at a moment's notice, even if he is in temporary vows. In the latter case, a short time must be allowed for the abbot to dispense his vows, but this only takes a matter of minutes. The only exception to this is if a monk is in life vows, when dispensation can take several months. Provided that the above rules are adhered to, the monk can leave quite honourably.

5

Community Activities

RETREAT

Just as the members of a community go out to conduct retreats, so the community holds its own annual retreat. The guest-house is closed for the week, which is a time for rest and rehabilitation. A short retreat can be recommended to all. Some communities make conducting retreats their speciality, or one can go privately to any community. A parish priest will gladly make arrangements.

Community retreats fall into two categories, the general annual retreat and the personal retreat before clothing or profession which is conducted by one's own superior. It has been suggested that the latter is intended to prevent one's relatives who attend the profession, from dissuading one from going through with it. Nothing is further from the truth. Candidates are actively encouraged not to proceed, so that only true vocations will be professed.

The general retreat starts after compline. No voice will then be heard, other than that of the retreat conductor until the retreat is over, except for the chanting of the office. The essential work of preparing meals must go on, but usually batches of suet puddings and pies are prepared beforehand and these along with cold dishes and hot soups are served to leave the minimum of kitchen work.

On the morning of the last day of the retreat, the conductor will sum up the retreat publicly and be available for private interview or hearing confessions. The atmosphere is happy and some conductors tell humorous anecdotes and experiences one of which I remember well— the retreat conductor said it was quite true. The priest of one of the Greater London parishes used to keep a black Labrador bitch which was in the habit of wandering into the church, if she could creep in unobserved. The animal rejoiced in the name of "Tessa" but the curates called her "Bitch" to which name she answered equally well. Being an Anglo-Catholic church, the priest was engaged in hearing confessions. Tessa wandered in, and the priest seeing her, said sharply, "Bitch! Go home!" and, immediately, one of the female penitents got up and walked out.

Episodes such as this will, I hope, dispel the illusion that all is gloom and despondency in a monastery.

After a brief summing-up talk from the retreat conductor, the conventual Mass usually follows before the community comes out of retreat. The guest-house fills up again, and the everyday life of the monastery continues.

Should any reader be interested in visiting or making a retreat at any monastery, a letter, in the first instance addressed to the guestmaster, will receive immediate attention. A stamped addressed envelope is a courtesy. Addresses of Anglican communities are given in Peter Anson's Book *The Call of the Cloister*, obtainable at most public libraries.

TELEVISION STARS
It is not often that a monastic community has the opportunity to appear on television, although this medium often uses monasteries as the setting for plays, frequently giving a grossly distorted image.

When a certain community was given the chance to appear in a documentary, it was delighted at the opportunity to present an authentic picture. The abbot briefed them before the television crew arrived. When the camera team did arrive, they came in a convoy of three large vans and special arrangements were made for the not inconsiderable number of technicians to stay in the monastery and to be fed in the refectory. The monks were told that they would be recompensed for any damage and payment would be made for the use of the premises when the programme went on the air.

From that time onwards, the crew treated the monastery like a film set. One could not go for a walk in the grounds without a camera and microphone popping up from nowhere and a voice instructing you to "Walk here. Walk there. Put your hood up," and many other requests. Cables ran everywhere and even the monk's cells were invaded. They wanted shots of monks in bed, studying, reading, in fact every aspect of monastic activity. They wanted shots of chapter in session, monks working in workshop and garden, and haymaking. The latter was quite phoney, as it was not even the haymaking season. They invaded the novitiate and filmed everywhere there. They wanted a shot of the abbot and novice master interviewing a new applicant, so a novice dressed in civilian clothes for the purpose.

They invaded the kitchens and filmed meals being prepared and took shots of the refectory at mealtime with the community processing in. If the camera had panned a little further along, it would have shown the monks gambolling over a pile of cables like a group of spring lambs.

Arriving in chapel for Mass, the monks even found the cameras set up there. The crew were forbidden to take shots of the actual consecration, but they settled for an abbreviated mock-up afterwards.

They took shots of hooded monks after compline, but to their eternal credit, they did observe the Greater Silence.

By this time the community was heartily sick of them and was pleased to see the vans pack up. The director expressed satisfaction with what he had got "in the can" and he went with thanks for their co-operation, leaving the monks ruefully surveying the tracks on the lawns, where the vans had ploughed across them. Subsequently, there was a cheque to cover damage which included a broken window.

The community was told that the programme would be shown on a certain night after the time they normally retired, and that about twenty minutes of the two hours material would be shown. Obviously some of the 'stars' would not appear.

The abbot arranged for the loan of a television set and

for everyone to come into the common-room in pyjamas and dressing-gowns after compline. As they entered, the previous programme was finishing and theirs started. After a few minutes, it appeared that their item was coming later. They watched the second and third item and the programme finished—they had been cut out altogether.

Subsequent enquiry elicited the information that the item was being held for future showing, but I have never heard of it being used. Surely someone would comment if they saw it. Many friends rang the monastery the next day asking what had happened.

The community felt that it had been used and the monks had lost two hours sleep which they could ill afford as they had to be up at 5.00 a.m. the following morning as usual.

I have never seen any shots of the monastery on television since, nor have I heard of the material being used, as I mentioned above. One would think that having spent good money on filming, and it must have cost quite a bit to bring all the men and equipment to the monastery, the television company would want to use the material. We heard nothing from them afterwards, except for the cheque for damage done, so we do not know if the film was a failure. Even if this were so, surely not all of the material would be useless?

6

Brother Matthew

Stephen Albert Quine was a clever boy and passed his School Certificate, as it was then, with several distinctions. He always avoided sports when possible, and kept himself apart from the other boys. As he became older, he never mixed with the girls of the nearby girl's school at school socials and dances, as the other older boys did. At the Christmas party, when one of the girls showed an interest in him, he shied away. The first realization came to him that he was different from the other boys. He had often heard the other boys making crude jokes about homosexuals and he began to wonder.

As he grew older, he shunned female society altogether and his relationship with other men was cautious. His religious upbringing prevented any experimentation and he retired into his shell completely and became a 'loner'.

His father, thinking he was ill, called in the family doctor to give him a check-up. Stephen, on a sudden impulse, decided to discuss his problem with the doctor who confirmed his worst fears.

From that time, Stephen resolved to withdraw himself from society and seek admission to the monastery at which he had made various retreats. He kept his secret to himself and managed to pass the medical conducted by the monastery doctor without giving himself away as his physical condition was good.

He served his postulancy and novitiate, being commended on his attainment in study and when he came up for life vows he easily obtained the necessary chapter votes. He was life professed and ordained, feeling a great relief that he had attained what he imagined was a safe haven.

It is well to comment here that he had entered the monastery from a wrong motive. The only true vocation is the desire to seek God, any other motive usually fails. Over the coming years, however, he discovered the right motive and consequently, happiness. He met his downfall owing to his being in a community of men.

A young postulant had occasion to visit his cell on quite legitimate business. The youngster was already showing signs of worldliness which go with a non-vocation. There was no question of his only sending the one letter allowed weekly. He procured stamps and posted extra letters surreptitiously during the Sunday afternoon walks. There were other such irregularities which together pointed to his rejection, for obedience in small matters leads to obedience in big ones.

No one except the professed monk and the postulant will ever know what took place, precisely. Suffice it to say that the master of studies, calling on Dom Matthew, found the two of them in the monk's bed.

The postulant was commanded to dress himself and was marched off to the abbot. Dom Matthew was advised to remain in his cell pending judgement.

Again, no one knows exactly what transpired, but the novice master was called in and the postulant confined to his cell. Dom Matthew was also summoned by the abbot and then sent back to his cell.

It was expected that the postulant would be sent away. Dom Matthew could not be dismissed without the decision of the advisory Council of Religious and the Bishops. The two were confined to their cells, food being sent up by the infirmarian.

No one knows how he managed it. Possibly he telephoned whilst the community was in chapel, but the postulant was met in reception by two young men who came in a car whilst the community was in chapel, and that was the last that was heard of him.

The monk? After a week's retreat, he once again appeared in the community. The juniors and lay brothers never knew details, only the life professed who sat in chapter did. But the general opinion was that the monk was more sinned against than sinning, more to be pitied than condemned. At any rate, the incident was forgotten and Dom Matthew continued to live an exemplary monastic life.

Two incidents in his later life are worth reporting. On one occasion, he was sent to hospital for eye treatment by a specialist. On leaving he was waiting for the monastery car, when another car pulled up. Dom Matthew noticed that its bumpers overhung the commencement of the double yellow line. He remembered one of the oblates being fined five pounds for this, and he indicated it to the driver, who thanked him for pointing it out. The driver then remarked that Dom Matthew did not come from these parts. He said he was interested in local dialects, and asked Dom Matthew if he would answer some questions? The driver then said that he could detect a trace of Staffordshire, also of West Midlands, probably Wolverhampton. This was remarkable, as the driver had detected his home county, and also the accent of Wolverhampton where he had been to boarding-school as a boy.

Dom Matthew congratulated the driver, and remarked that he would make a good Professor Higgins. They were laughing over this, when the monastery car arrived. I had always regarded the incident in *Pygmalion* as fanciful until this was related to me.

The other incident occurred when Dom Matthew went to relieve in a parish. One of the local clergy called upon a bed-ridden old lady of over ninety years. Her end was approaching, although she was quite lucid. She explained that she was quite ready to find her rest on the bosom of Isaac.

"Surely you mean the bosom of Abraham," said the priest. The old lady replied, "Young man, if you had been an old maid as long as I have, you would not be particular on which male bosom you took your rest!"

What caused Dom Matthew to succumb on the occasion mentioned earlier, we shall never know. Presumably it was the actions of the youngster involved. Dom Matthew was a very likeable person normally and there had never been any unpleasantness involving him before, not has there been since.

His unfortunate trait was of course known to the community by the time of the incident, as he freely admitted it. He was, however, very much in control of himself.

7

Some Questions Answered

The reader, having borne with me thus far will no doubt, if not conversant with a religious community, have several questions to ask.

In this chapter I propose to answer the questions most frequently put to me.

Why do we wear our peculiar habit? This was the dress of the working man when the orders were founded, and it is still worn, traditionally. This is also why priests wear their vestments at Mass. In this case, it was the dress of the nobility when they attended Mass. Our habit is virtually unchanged, although the scapular, mentioned before, used to be worn as an overall for work. Likewise the cowl of the life professed used to be fleece-lined for warmth. Now, in these days of central heating, it is very thin.

The habit can give rise to odd incidents. One of our monks once got his scapular caught in the doors of an underground train, and was dragged along as it was too thin to prevent the doors from closing. He managed to slip his head out, and a passenger pulled the communication cord and stopped the train.

Two of our monks were waiting at a station alongside several youngsters dressed as teddy boys. The youngsters were obviously fascinated by the habits, and one of them asked what they were. One of the monks seeing the possibility of a joke, said that this was the very latest 'gear', that the teddy boys were out of date, and should 'get with it'. This rather nonplussed the youngster, who withdrew with his group, presumably to discuss whether they were being teased or not.

We are often told that the monastic life is a waste of time, particularly the 'useless' chanting of the Psalms. I can only quote St Augustine, "If the psalm prays, then pray. If it entreats then entreat. If it is glad, rejoice. If it expresses hope, then hope. If fear, then fear. For all that is here written is like the mirror of your own experience." The Psalms were the worship of the Jews, out of which Christian worship was born. I was told an anecdote concerning this. No doubt there is a moral somewhere.

A devout Jew went to his rabbi in considerable agitation. He said, "I am mortified to admit that my son has become a Christian." The rabbi replied, "I am also mortified to admit that my son also has become a Christian." They decided to consult the Chief Rabbi, who said, "Now that is a remarkable coincidence. My son also has become a Christian." After discussion, they decided to pray to Jehovah for guidance. When their prayer finished, the voice of Jehovah came from Heaven, saying, "Now that is a remarkable coincidence. . . ."

There are people (for example journalists and authors) who wish to learn more about monasteries for reasons other than religion. One such was a student studying for a higher degree in Social Studies, who selected monastic life as part of his thesis. On his first visit I let him interview me, along with other monks. He took copious notes about my domestic and social background, school, university qualifications and so on. Then he started a series of questions to find out what motivates a monk.

One question concerned my opinion of my abbot and late novice master. When I replied that they were both outstanding examples to follow in one's monastic vocation, he replied, "Ha! Just what I expected. We have a name in psychology for this over-zealous opinion of one's superiors."

I told him bluntly not to be an ass. This was a candid opinion of two very worthy men, not a case for psychological interpretation. I too had studied psychology and knew what I was talking about.

On his second visit, he asked to see those monks whom

he had seen before, but I was not available—there was no point in wasting his time and mine.

Another sore point is the question of Monastic silence. It is irksome to the novice, but when one gets used to it one can see its usefulness. The sole purpose of the silence is to enable the monk to live prayerfully in the presence of God. Silence is the best way of accomplishing this. It is as simple as that.

Sometimes visitors are confused by seeing monks conversing freely at times and at other times refraining from speech to the extent of using sign language. In the liberal Benedictine observance, speech is not totally banned except during the Greater Silence, or where it might disturb others. Speech is free on feast days (*dies non*) and on long recreations such as Sunday afternoons.

The burning question—should monks smoke?

I gave it up some ten years before entering, so I speak unbiased. A lady visitor who had been a modest benefactress of the monastery was scandalized to see a monk smoking. When told that this was in order, she said she would stop her contributions, as she was not prepared to see her money "go up in smoke".

There is nothing about this in the Rule of course, since St Benedict preceded tobacco by several hundred years. However, alcohol, a similar worldly habit, is mentioned. A small ration of wine, he allows, although "abstention brings its own reward".

As stated previously, the ration of tobacco is minute by worldly standards and alcohol is only allowed in strict moderation on major feast days, when beer or wine is provided with meals.

Why do we submit to poverty, chastity and obedience? In about A.D.358 St Basil formulated his famous Rule and in A.D.530 Benedict wrote his amended Rule, based on that of Basil. Both Rules prescribe poverty, chastity, and obedience.

Poverty is prescribed because the monastery does much

work for the poor and underprivileged and the monks, existing on alms and their own earnings, have little left after their philanthropic activities.

Chastity is rather the result of poverty, than of leaving oneself unattached for the work of God. One could not afford to maintain a wife under monastic conditions. We are often told that chastity is unnatural. Probably so, yet many people in the world live a chaste life. A monk has four years to decide if he can observe this before life profession. There have been occasional failures and scandals, but not as many as people imagine.

Obedience is essential as the system demands that all pull together under one person's directions.

Regarding the vexed question of fasting, some people imagine that monks spend all their time fasting, yet have you ever seen an undernourished monk?

The canonical fast consists of frugality rather than abstinence. During fasting times such as Lent, breakfast is a Continental-style meal. Lunch is the normal full meal but tea consists of a drink only as the usual bread and jam are omitted. The evening meal is one full course only with cocoa or lemonade to drink. No meat is served on Mondays, Wednesdays or Fridays. None of this is any real hardship. The exception is Good Friday when lunch consists of a scrambled egg on one round of buttered toast, then one goes hungry until the evening meal, usually a large helping of fish pie. This fast is only followed by those who have been passed as fit and it does not apply to anyone under twenty-one or over sixty.

I shall anticipate the next question. No, we do not employ a chef. The monks do all the cooking. The breakfast cook has a refectorian to lay the tables. The lunch cook has two scullions to wash up after the breakfast cook and do odd jobs. This team also deals with pigswill and refuse in the afternoon, prepares meals for 'wayfarers' (tramps) and produces the urn at tea-time. The refectorian cuts bread and lays the tables for tea as well as for lunch and dinner. The dinner cook works alone and leaves his washing up for the scullions.

A sample menu might consist of:

Breakfast	Fried bacon or egg or sausage Tea or coffee
Lunch	Liver and onions Steamed raisin pudding and custard Water
Tea	Bread, butter and jam Tea
Dinner	Vegetable soup Cottage pie Cocoa

The food is nourishing if institutional. Cooking varies from bad to excellent according to the cook.

What about the tonsure? Some communities have a normal haircut and some have the tonsure with the "hole in the middle", an adaptation of the shaven head of the penitent. Most have a crew cut for reasons of hygiene and because it can be cut by the monks themselves.

Why are monks' cells so bare? Mainly because of the vow of poverty. It would cost a fortune to carpet cell floors. Two sheets, two pillows, three blankets, an under-blanket and a coverlet are provided. One clean sheet and one clean pillow-case are supplied fortnightly and the top sheet is put to the bottom with the clean sheet on top. The cell is centrally heated, except in late spring, summer and early autumn. When cold, one studies in one's cloak.

One is not allowed to move furniture around, and a photograph of one's parents is the only personal item allowed.

8

Brother Anthony

Ronald Edward Percy Woolley was the son of a Lancashire cotton magnate. His grandfather was elevated to the peerage for public beneficence and since in those days the title was hereditary, our entrant would have inherited title and estate.

He could never become a monk because his wife still lived, separated from him. He did well to fit in as a lowly oblate, considering his background and Eton and Cambridge education.

He had become entangled with a barmaid while at Cambridge and eventually married the girl. This caused a family row and he would have been disinherited but for the intervention of his mother. He lost his seat on the board of the family business and left to make his own way in business.

Having wrecked his career, his wife, finding that money had become scarce, ran off with another man. Ronald applied to join the monastery but found it difficult for one can never enter on the rebound. He still had a legal wife, although fortunately there was no issue. There was no maintenance problem, as his mother had given the girl money on condition that she lived abroad with her gentleman friend. If they had married, this would have left Ronald free to enter the monastery, but, knowing this, his wife had no intention of making things easy for him.

Rejected as a postulant, Ronald applied to enter as a claustral oblate and was accepted. A year and a day after entry, he made his life promises (not vows).

After two years he was assistant to the guestmaster and a familiar figure amongst the guests with his habit and short knee-length scapular without a hood.

He was popular in the community, but, being absent-minded, became the object of the pranks of the youngsters. This he accepted with good humour, which increased his popularity.

Often, on feast days in the monastery, visiting priests from the nearby Roman convent were entertained. They joined us in our common-room and similarities and differences between Romanism and Anglicanism were discussed. They thought that our Anglo-Catholic observance was more Catholic than that of Rome. We only differed in recognizing Canterbury instead of Rome as our head, and because of the similarity between the two, Anglo-Catholics often defect to Rome and vice versa.

In conversation with the Roman priests, Brother Anthony wondered if he were in the right communion. Since he was so close to Rome, why should he not go all the way?

Personally, I see no reason to desert the faith of my birth, unless the Anglican Church were to do something silly like attempting to ordain women, which is a contradiction in terms and theologically impossible.

However, Brother Anthony finally convinced himself and joined the Roman communion. There was no coercion and it was entirely his own decision. The last I heard was that he had been dispensed from his promises by our abbot and had settled as a claustral oblate in a Roman Catholic monastery.

9

Disciplinary Measures

It will be appreciated that, human nature being what it is, the odd bad egg in a large consignment is bound to appear. This happens in any walk of life and the Church is no exception.

The remarkable thing is that 'murder' can be committed in other walks of life without a ripple of comment. In the Church it is quite a different matter. A grossly underpaid curate has only to succumb to the temptation to 'borrow' some of the parish funds and all the hounds of hell are on his tail. Not that the action of the said cleric can be condoned, but the general public are always ready to pounce on him, whereas they would wink at the offence and let it pass from someone in another walk of life, who would be able to help himself to quite a lot without comment, on the grounds that it was part of the 'perks' of the job. For this reason, the cleric must not only be scrupulously honest, but must manifestly be seen to be so.

As for crimes involving sex, the public is always ready to try, convict, and extort the maximum penalty from any member of the Church, whilst we hear of many cases of 'wife-swapping' parties outside. Our Lord himself was willing to forgive the woman caught in the act of adultery, and He suggested that her accusers search their own consciences before condemning her, however, He did not condone her act.

Partly due to public outcry, but mostly to keep its own house in order, the Church has to find the means of dealing with the odd defaulter, so that its good name is upheld. The public outcry is probably only a mob reaction against one of its species who has set his sights high, and come to grief. The fall is thus magnified.

I would emphasize here that statistics show that the percentage of criminal proceedings against members of the Church, is infinitesimal in comparison with cases outside the Church, which is as it should be.

After the law has dealt with an offender, the Church must in turn deal with him and this is often accomplished by using the monasteries.

In the case of what may be called "crimes of scandal" which are not punishable by law, they are dealt with by the Church, usually with the news media in full cry. The offender is suspended from duty immediately and if the offence is not serious enough for him to be unfrocked and expelled from the Church, he is often sent to a monastery for a few months to give him a chance to ruminate upon his sins.

The monasteries do occasionally have such an offender staying with them, but I must emphasize that in all the monasteries with which I was conversant, both Roman and Anglican, in my seven years in a community I only came across two such cases. Considering the number of people involved in the two denominations, it must be agreed that this is a very good record.

When an offender is to be admitted to a monastery, the community is usually briefed beforehand by the abbot, so that no one makes a *faux pas* in conversation with the offender, who will be mixing with them in the senior common-room. The full details of the cases are not disclosed, but only the information necessary so that they can deal charitably with the offender.

It must be remembered that monks are not in contact with the news media to the same extent as the general public. However, there is generally a place set aside for copies of the better newspapers, known as "newspaper corner" and there is also some means of monitoring the radio news, so that important news may be imparted to the monks, usually on the notice-board.

To digress, news during election times is freely posted. Contrary to general opinion, monks do vote at elections and the election manifestos of all parties are available to them. Some are even allowed to attend party meetings, but they must not speak on the subject. It will be appreciated that it is desirable for monks to have a say in policy if they are to pray for those policies. Come election day, the monks are taken by car to vote.

When an offending cleric arrives in the monastery, he lives and works with the community. He celebrates Mass along with the other ordained members of the community, unless he has been barred from so doing by his suspension. He is offered all the rights and privileges of his rank in the Church. If his case has attracted too much undesirable comment, he sits with the community instead of at the guest table, to save embarrassment during meals, when talking is permitted.

In the chapel, he sits with the community or if a bishop, he will occupy the bishop's throne. If the terms of his suspension resulted in temporary demotion, a bishop would be treated as an ordinary priest, unless excommunicated as well. An excommunicated priest cannot celebrate Mass or even receive communion.

I hasten to point out that all clerics living in the monastery are not under a cloud. Some are recuperating after illness, in which case their work contribution is adjusted accordingly. There are also some priest oblates who live in the monastery permanently if, for example, their health would not permit them to pass the rigorous medical examination required to become a monk.

It must also be remembered that some clerics are in the monastery for offences which would pass without comment in the outside world. For example, one of the two cases which I have mentioned above was in the monastery under suspension because he had sworn at his bishop, unfortunately, in front of one of his churchwardens. Whilst this behaviour cannot be condoned, it was probable that his bishop deserved to be sworn at, I have known some bishops who could be very exasperating.

Apart from a floating population of outside parish priests temporarily living in the monastery, there are also many visiting clergy, oblates and others, who come to the monastery either to make a retreat under the guidance of one of the monks, or just for a short holiday, away from the cares of running a parish. The monastery is an ideal spot for a total rest of this kind.

10

A Choir Monk and
Two Lay Brothers

BROTHER JOSEPH

Lawrence Warwick John Tyler had all the advantages
which a young man could wish to launch him into the
world. He came from a wealthy family, his father being the
owner of a nationwide chain of textile factories which
earned millions of pounds per annum. The father saw the
slump coming and had sufficient business acumen to pull
out of the enterprise, before the lean years started. He
retired and bought a villa in the south of France, where he
lived during the winter months. The children had the
advantage of the best education that money could buy, the
two girls being sent to Roedean, followed by a finishing
school in Switzerland. Lawrence went to Harrow and
Oxford.

Lawrence had always been interested in physics,
particularly the new field of nuclear physics. He obtained
an Honours degree in science and stayed on at Oxford for
his Ph.D. By the age of thirty he had become a leading
authority on nuclear physics, with several books to his
credit. He was married only to his work.

When war came, Lawrence was well established at what
later became Harwell Atomic Research Station and he
was not called up because of this. He was so engrossed in
his work that he never considered the ethics of using
atomic energy. The Americans, of course, claimed the in-
vention of the atomic bomb but Lawrence knew where the
spade-work had been done and he was part of the team
that went to the States to provide the 'know-how'. It was

not until Hiroshima and Nagasaki that he considered the ethics of his work.

Lawrence questioned the justification for using the bombs and he felt personally responsible. His friends argued, quite rightly, that the bomb shortened the war and saved many Allied as well as Japanese lives, for the Japanese sold their lives dearly as the Allies approached their homeland.

Lawrence brooded on the issue for some weeks and found it quite a traumatic experience. Then an idea dawned upon him. He had neglected his religion for years, but perhaps the Church could help him. He therefore went to the nearest church to seek the advice of the priest.

As luck would have it, this was an Anglo-Catholic church, and the priest was on duty, hearing confessions. Lawrence waited with the others and took his turn to kneel beside the priest as they had done. He said frankly, "I have neglected the Church for years, but a crisis has arisen which is tearing me apart. Will you help me?"

The priest said he would help willingly, but he suggested that it would be better discussed over a cup of coffee at the priest house. He blessed Lawrence and asked him to wait until he had heard the remaining two confessions.

Accordingly, with a tray of coffee between them, Lawrence poured out his story. This conversation brought about a friendship that lasted for life and also resulted in the conversion of Lawrence, who discovered the missing part of his life.

Lawrence abandoned his scientific job and thinking that his conversion was a call to the ministry, he entered a theological college. The study came easily to him and he gained his General Ordination Certificate and also a diploma in theology. He asked for and obtained a curacy in London's dockland where he performed yeoman service amongst the criminals, drug addicts and alcoholics. Here, he made his first contacts with the monastery, as the monks were also engaged on this work.

Well-wishers obtained a living for him in the smart area of Harrogate but Lawrence refused it and so gave offence. He knew he must put himself out of reach, or it would happen again and he saw the monastery as a way of achieving this. Why not join the monastery and continue his dockland ministry from there?

Lawrence applied for permission to enter, and was astounded when the abbot, having heard his story, turned him down. The abbot had seen Lawrence's ulterior motive and sent him away to reconsider. Lawrence tried again some six months later but the abbot said frankly that he had seen through his request. He could only accept him if he came unconditionally and he could not guarantee then that he would be sent to work in dockland.

Having slept on the problem, Lawrence asked for unconditional entry the following day, and was accepted. He settled his patrimony upon his sisters and finding them a smaller establishment, as it happened near the abbey, he disposed of the family estates in England and France. Impulsively, he wanted to give the proceeds to the abbey, but was told that this was not possible until he was life professed.

The postulancy was a difficult time for Lawrence as he was used to giving orders, not taking them. He was accepted for clothing as a novice but, as Brother Joseph, he found himself in a peculiar position. As a priest he celebrated daily Mass, but he was not allowed to celebrate conventual Mass until in vows. At Mass he was Father Joseph in control of the situation, afterwards he was Brother Joseph, the most junior of the novices. The situation was explosive. It is well known that priests find the monastic life harder to adapt to than laymen.

Obviously the novice master could not teach him much about theology. His list of qualifications was a formidable one, the Revd. Doctor Tyler, B.Sc.,Ph.D.,Dip.Theol., and having to take orders from boys of eighteen was a severe exercise in self-effacement. It was at this time that he developed the 'lone wolf' attitude which characterized him ever after.

He won through to temporary profession through sheer grit. After a year in temporary vows, his mother died and he was allowed to attend the funeral and see his sisters settled. Returning to the monastery, he settled to the hard work again. His hands became toughened by using spade and shovel and he did his kitchen duties without complaint.

It was as second scullion that his hardest trial came. There was a lay brother who regularly took the evening cooking duty and delighted in making the lives of the juniors miserable. After cooking, this lay brother would dump plates and pans in the washing tank with uneaten food on them. He then turned on the cold water and left the filthy mess for Brother Joseph to sort out.

Requests to place the pots and pans on a side table were ignored. Brother Joseph had to remove them and scour out the revolting mess before he could start. Complaints to the novice master produced no results because the lay brother was of longer standing service than the novice master. It was Brother Joseph's cross and he would have to bear it. The lay brother taunted him that he had not the determination to become a monk and he nearly gave up and left. However, he clenched his teeth and endured it and learnt the bitter lesson of ignoring the persecution. At last, the lay brother, realizing that he no longer irritated Brother Joseph, desisted.

After finishing the first two years in temporary vows, Brother Joseph was invited to join the senior commonroom, and some of the more onerous duties were relaxed a little. He had nearly made the grade, and he began to enjoy life. His sisters, who had bought a little car, were now allowed to visit him on Sundays and he had tea with them in guest reception. On the alternate weeks when they did not visit him, he spent his spare time walking alone in the grounds. He was rebuked for this and told that during Long Recreations, he should associate more with his brethren. He made the effort, but he was happier alone.

The time arrived for his election to life vows and he was astounded when the chapter recommended another year in temporary vows. He found that he would have to be more of an extrovert in order to attain life vows. At the end of the year, he managed to get the necessary votes and was life professed at forty-eight—a late vocation.

His anxiety was over, but he had reached the most

trying time, when a monk has nothing more to strive for. This 'deflation' period is why the Church allows secularization even after life vows if necessary.

He was now beyond the reach of the tormenting lay brother. Indeed he found that others had suffered at the hands of this man.

Dom Joseph entered into the full functions of a priest of the community. He had more sense than to ask, but he was overjoyed when he was sent to his beloved dockland.

He built up quite a reputation as a retreat conductor also and was in demand outside the monastery. He had a great sense of humour, and incorporated many anecdotes into his retreat addresses. Perhaps it would not be out of place to repeat one of them here.

A happily married couple died together, as they had always wished, and went to Heaven. St Peter, who greeted them, remarked that they had been through a hard time on earth and they could have one wish to compensate them. The husband spoke up and said that as they were so poor they had been unable to have the elegant wedding which his wife had longed for. Could they be remarried in Heaven, with all the trappings that they had missed? Peter promised to arrange it.

A thousand years passed and still no wedding had taken place. They ventured to remind Peter who said, "Not to worry. I never forget a promise."

Another thousand years passed before Peter announced that all was arranged. There was to be a full nuptial Mass, followed by a gigantic reception with all the company of Heaven as guests. Peter apologized for the delay which was caused by having to await the arrival of a priest in Heaven!

Dom Joseph was renowned for his pertinent quotations. One favourite was French, *"L'obliger à dire 'Oui' sans mais, sans si, sans pourquoi à toutes les volontés de Dieu"*. (The obligation to say "Yes", without but, without if, without why, to all the wishes of God.) Another was, "The Benedictine Order is enclosed, but some monks struggle to find excuses to absent themselves from the monastery. I suppose they suffer from 'cloister-phobia'."

The years passed happily, and the Silver Jubilee of his ordination and profession passed by. These were occasions of great rejoicing, and his friends and relatives gathered to see him celebrate Mass on each occasion.

Shortly afterwards, the abbot appointed him sub-prior, which forced him into closer contact with his brethren. The ploy succeeded and he mellowed greatly.

He reached his seventieth birthday, remaining marvellously fit and active, until he started to suffer from gastric problems. The infirmarian sent him for medical treatment and he was put on a strict low-roughage diet and forbidden stalky cabbage and chunky marmalade amongst other things, which gave rise to a humorous incident. Normally the community had cheap marmalade, but at feast times they had special chunky marmalade, of which he was passionately fond. One 'talking' feast-day breakfast, Dom Joseph reached out for the 'Chunky', thinking the infirmarian had not seen him. As he picked it up, the infirmarian said, "Remember your diet!"

Dom Joseph exploded "The only time when we get Christian marmalade and I must have the sloppy stuff!" From that time chunky marmalade was known as "Christian marmalade" in the community.

Dom Joseph's condition deteriorated. He lost weight, and the doctor sent him to hospital for observation. We were all shocked when the specialist diagnosed cancer of the bowel. He had now reached his eightieth year. The specialist wished to operate, but Dom Joseph objected. The specialist did not insist for eighty is a good age.

He returned to the community in care of the infirmarian, presumably to die. Prayers were offered and Masses said for him. He was the patriarch of the monastery and popular despite his abrupt manner. He was in bed for three months and became more cheerful daily. The doctor examined him regularly and was puzzled because the growth was not now palpable so Dom Joseph was returned to hospital for X-ray examination. There was no doubt about it, the growth had receded.

Power of prayer? Miracle? The medical textbooks tell us that such improvement can happen in old people. We grow by cell division and cancer is only cell division running out of control. In the elderly, normal cell division runs down and it can counteract the abnormal cell division of cancer, resulting in regression of the tumour.

This is what happened to Dom Joseph and he was on his feet before the year was out. He was dispensed from the office by the abbot and told to come and go as he pleased. Everyone said he would outlive us all.

One wet Corpus Christi, visitors were admitted more freely to the enclosure, out of the rain. At Mass the overflow spread to the choir stalls. Dom Joseph had not turned up, and the abbot allowed a lady to occupy his stall, just as he appeared having been at prayer in the Lady Chapel. As soon as he saw the lady in his stall he let out a snort which was heard all over the chapel, and stomped off back to the Lady Chapel. The abbot smiled. Anyone else would have been reprimanded.

Not many years later Dom Joseph was confined to bed. He was feeble but still eating like a horse. Everyone willed him to reach his ninetieth birthday and the monks had a celebration when this happened. The workshop staff made him a present—a bookrest, as he could not hold a book in bed.

He lasted two more years before he succumbed. His sisters, no longer able to drive, were fetched by the monastery car for the funeral. A large number of guests, unknown to the community came, many from the dockland parish. Even an old Harwell colleague, a sprightly eighty-nine-year-old, turned up.

Some of the juniors called him a misogynist, remembering the Corpus Christi incident, but we who had known him for years, knew that this was only an inherent shyness.

Dom Joseph was the monk who, having been laid low in the great Asian 'flu epidemic which caused three-quarters of the inhabitants of the monastery to take to their beds, tried to shoo out of his cell, the female doctor and the District Nurse, who had come to attend him. This episode is mentioned in a later chapter.

A Choir Monk and Two Lay Brothers

BROTHER IGNATIUS

William Stokes was a lonely boy. Born of a Bristol family, there is no record of the occupation of his father who died when William was twelve. William attended a church school and had an Anglo-Catholic upbringing but he was somewhat retarded. He spent his spare time wandering in the dock area and longed to be free of school and to go to sea. His life changed when his mother died just before he was fourteen and the local vicar put him in the care of a convent.

William left the convent and stowed away in one of the lifeboats of a ship about to sail. He knew if he could remain hidden until the pilot was dropped, the captain would let him work his passage if he said he was fourteen. He kept under cover by day and crept out at night to reconnoitre. The second night, fast asleep, he was awoken by the ship's alarm bells signalling a regulation lifeboat drill. William was discovered when the crew removed the boat cover, and marched off to the bridge. He was fascinated by the ship's officers giving orders to cover the 'emergency' as the crew assembled in life-jackets.

The drill completed, the captain dealt with William who maintained that he was over fourteen, and had no relatives and wanted to go to sea. The captain radioed his company offices and agreed to sign William on as crew. He would act as cabin boy and be paid on completion of the round trip.

After being 'paid off' at Bristol eighteen months later, the next we hear of William is that at the age of twenty-seven he had found himself a job as a steward on a P & O liner, based at Southampton. He never discussed the intervening years, but presumably he had more experience at sea.

However, we find him setting out on a Mediterranean cruise. He was an assistant steward at the bar in a passenger lounge. The work was hard, as he served drinks and collected 'empties' from 10.00 a.m. until the small hours. He could spend his off-duty days ashore when the ship was in port since the ship's bars were closed due to local excise regulations.

On one such occasion, the ship stood off the island of Elba which had no port with sufficient draught. Most of the passengers were ashore and William was amusing himself fishing from the landing-stage which was lowered for the launches.

He became conscious of someone watching him, and a cultured voice enquired if he had caught anything. Looking up, he recognized a passenger whom he had served. William explained the varieties of fish available and showed his catch.

The passenger seemed interested and enquired if William was married and what had made him come to sea. William opened out inexplicably, more than was his wont. Eventually, the passenger said he must find his wife, who had stayed aboard, sunbathing, and he departed.

Later in the cruise, the passenger asked William if he would be interested in a job as a general handyman on his estate. He employed a butler, a housekeeper, a gardener, and a general factotum, who had just died. William's duties would be maintenance work under the direction of the butler and he would act as wine waiter when they had guests. There were also two cars which he would clean and polish. The employers had no chauffeur as they preferred to drive themselves. William would live in and the wage offered was very attractive.

When William finally accepted, he was given directions to find the estate and told to make his way there when paid off from the ship.

On leaving the train at the nearest country station, William enquired about transport. The porter laughed and said it was 'shank's pony' unless he waited two hours for the local carrier. As it was five miles to the estate William preferred to wait rather than walk that distance with his suitcase.

The carrier turned up in an ancient van with "Arkwright Carrier" painted on its side, drawn by an equally ancient horse. He agreed to take William for the sum of half a crown.

On arrival, William was dumped at the end of a long drive leading to a manor-house. The extensive grounds were flanked by a high wall on one side and a lane on the other. On the right was a large flower garden, on the left was woodland. The house itself was a double-bayed edifice and, as William deemed it unwise to approach the front door, he went round to the back, after traversing the large circular rose-bed outside the front door, which the drive surrounded. He found the back door with another wing flanking it, and rang the bell. Out popped an elderly man in tail-coat—obviously the butler. He barked, "You are Stokes. We expected you earlier. Follow me." They traversed a corridor and passed through a green baize door into the servants' quarters. Along another corridor, the butler flung open a door, disclosing a plainly furnished but comfortable single bedroom—William's new home.

We will not describe William's work there. He was fed and housed comfortably, the pay was generous and William enjoyed his work. Every year the servants were sent to a monastery or convent for a week's retreat in addition to their week's holiday with pay.

It was thus that William first encountered the monastery. After two years, realizing that his employer was getting old and thinking of the future, he applied for admission to the monastery. He turned on his charm and was admitted as a lay postulant.

William managed to behave himself and was ultimately admitted to life profession as a lay brother. As we find him in the monastery, he is fairly advanced in years and adept at avoiding arduous duties.

His work-dodging was finally noticed and his position investigated. In his cell were found a radio, cine projector, radiogram and electric blanket. It was discovered that he had tricked young entrants into handing over possessions to him. Nominally in charge of the laundry, he had shuffled the work on to juniors. He had obtained control of the three bicycles belonging to the monastery, and spent long periods out on them without permission. He also had a complete set of civilian clothes, which had been given to the monastery, and he had altered them to fit him.

All this came to light when he was challenged regarding his infrequent attendance at communion and confession.

It had only gone on this long because monks must not criticize others but should confess their faults voluntarily. Brother Ignatius was devoid of a vocation and had omitted to do so.

I hasten to say that this was the only case that I discovered like this. He was the one bad egg in the consignment.

The sequel was that his case was discussed in chapter, pending a decision on him, but the question of disciplinary action never arose, since Brother Ignatius disappeared whilst his case was under consideration. He was never heard of in the monastery again. Nobody knew where he went and enquiries were not pressed too far. It was probably the best solution in the end.

Most likely he would have been sent to another monastery of the order, but certainly he would never have been able to feather his nest like this again.

Cases such as his are virtually unknown today, although many years ago, the whole Benedictine order, or Black Monks, as they were called, had fallen into negligent habits and laxity of observance, until St Bernard reformed the monastery at Cisterce, out of which the so-called White Monks, or Cistercians were founded.

BROTHER SYLVESTER
Claude James Pegg was the son of a dental surgeon from Norfolk. He was one of those unusual entrants who wish to enter the lay brotherhood although he had the necessary academic qualifications to enter as a choir monk.

Although his father was pressing him to follow in the family dental practice, it soon become evident that Claude would have none of it. His great love was engineering, particularly aero-engineering, and if his father had agreed to apprentice him to an aero-engineering firm, we should probably never have seen him in the monastery.

This was immediately prior to the Second World War, and the boy, leaving school at the age of seventeen years, had gained his School Certificate, but with not enough passes to obtain entrance into Edinburgh University where his father intended him to study dentistry. He was therefore sent back to the expensive but minor public school for another year to get his matriculation exemption.

The war broke out soon after his return to school, and a year's 'phoney' war dragged on. Likewise Claude dragged himself through the school year.

When he left school, this time with matriculation exemption, he was just eighteen years of age, and his father and the university authorities were pressing for permission for him to complete his university course before call-up.

Claude settled it himself by volunteering as a pilot in the R.A.F. He passed his medical and went on the usual wartime crash course, coming first in his class of officer cadets.

He was commissioned as Flying Officer James Pegg, tactfully dropping the Claude and was the life and soul of the Officer's Mess. He was quickly in action, flying Spitfires in the Battle of Britain and he totted up his flying hours the hard way—in combat. He maintained that aerial combat was a science, not an art. If one dived out of the sun, demolished one's target and got away quickly, one lived to fight another day. He finished the Battle of Britain with the rank of Flight Lieutenant and a tunic covered in 'gongs'. His only near miss was when a Messerschmidt pilot hit his Spitfire in a vital spot, but his luck held and he got away with a pancake or belly landing in which he sustained a broken leg. He was dragged out of the plane, which fortunately did not burst into flames. He had earned his six weeks' rest with his leg in plaster.

On rejoining his unit, much to his disgust but the thankfulness of his parents, he was sent to the United States as an instructor to train British pilots, where he remained for the rest of the war.

When the war was over, his father expected that he would start his dental studies, but Claude was a move ahead of him and applied for entrance to the monastery. His family was Anglo-Catholic and he had often made a retreat there. He persisted in his desire to enter as a lay brother.

His only interest apart from engineering, was languages. He spoke French fluently, and more than a little German, Spanish and Italian.

He served his term as a postulant and was admitted to the lay novitiate without incident. He was delighted when he was eventually put to work in the workshops and spent hours working with the big metal lathe, turning out the metal parts required by the workshop and metal sconces for candlesticks.

There was a donkey engine which worked the pumps which pumped the sewage uphill from the underground tanks to the distribution sprinkler at the top of the fields belonging to the monastery. Brother Sylvester was instrumental in getting this donkey engine changed for an electric motor, when it gave trouble. He also organized the laying of the electric cable underground and the connection of the electric motor. The only cost to the community was that of inspection by the Electricity Board, before the installation was connected to the mains.

Just before Brother Sylvester took his life vows, the master of juniors discovered his interest in languages. Accordingly, when he entered vows, a set of "Linguaphone" records in the four languages was purchased to assist his study. The master of juniors had recognized a born linguist and decided to encourage him. This paid off in later years when visitors from abroad came to the monastery. There were other linguists in the monastery, but he was always with them whenever possible, improving his accent and vocabulary.

With English, French, German, Spanish and Italian at his command, he was not often beaten until a party from Portugal arrived.

There was one humorous incident. He had to be admitted to hospital with severe abdominal pains. Whilst the specialist was examining him, one particularly bad spasm of pain afflicted him and Brother Sylvester let out an involuntary "Oh my God", and then realizing what he had said, explained that this was a prayer and not an imprecation. The specialist replied, "That's all right, old man. I realized that was what it was!"

His latent sense of humour came out during a discussion
on patron saints of workers. Some were obvious, as St
Joseph, patron of carpenters. Brother Sylvester said the
patron saint of commercial travellers and salesmen was
also obvious—Francis of Sales.

He was rather accident prone. He fell downstairs on one
occasion and fractured his arm. After having it set at the
local hospital, he was unable to participate in any work, so
he was given *carte blanche* for the six weeks that his arm
would be in plaster. He used a typewriter to write letters
with one hand.

During this time he wrote for us a rather 'corny' poem.
This is worth reproducing here since it does indicate to the
reader the sequence of the monastic time-table:

The Postulant's Guide to the Monastery Time-table

At five o'clock at the crack of dawn,
The ringer starts his round,
ringing the early rising bell,
a sweet and joyous sound!

On the first note of the bell,
we all leap out of bed.
We never think of staying put,
for forty winks instead!

At half past five on a shining morn,
we start our little day.
Matins and lauds and Low Mass,
we begin to say.

At seven o'clock, the breakfast bell.
The hungry gather round,
for coffee, bread, and marmalade,
and 'bangers' I'll be bound!

Then back to cell for private prayer,
and spiritual reading.
We carry on without a care,
The world the more receding.

Brothers of Habit

The next bell rings at eight o'clock.
We hurry down for prime,
the while we're quietly wondering
what happened to our time.

Nine twenty-five, 'tis time for terce
and conventual Mass.
After that you must turn out
for manual work, alas!

At twelve o'clock the angelus,
followed by sext and none.
Before we have our dinner thus,
we for our sins atone.

At half past twelve 'tis dinner time.
Our meal we most desire;
When "Table server, you, my lad!"
we hear from Father prior.

When one o'clock at last comes round,
siesta time is spent.
When work bell rings at two o'clock,
we wonder where time went!

We work throughout the afternoon—
workmaster's working squad.
If we should pause to take our breath,
he seems to think it odd!

Three forty-five, 'tis vespers time,
followed up by tea.
If you want the cup that cheers,
just come along with me.

After tea, 'tis study time,
(Latin and all that tack).
The novice master's always there
to see that you don't slack!

Six twenty-five, the call to prayer,
according to the Rule
laid down by Holy Benedict
for his "beginner's school".

Supper time at seven o'clock.
A most delicious stew,
made just like mother used to make,
by Brother Denys or Andrew.

Then comes recreation time.
We talk of many things;
The vernacular and Series Two,
and cabbages and kings.

At eight-thirty, the compline bell
calls once again to prayers.
Then Major Silence. After that
we're trotting up the stairs.

Then private prayers, and so to bed.
Please do not think it sad,
to turn in at this early hour.
You'll be thankful lad!

With apologies for corny verse.
It really has no charm.
It was a Brother's effort when
he had a broken arm.

If you should think for writing this,
he deserves a broken neck,
I pray you, gentle reader, please
to hold yourself in check!

Previously I have written prose,
to which I'm not averse.
My prose is very bad
you see, but this is verse!

Had his arm not been in plaster, he would have got all that
the brethren threatened for this effort!

Brother Sylvester was something of a rarity, since he
never had aspirations to change over to choir monk. Generally today, entrants will struggle to assimilate the
necessary Greek and Latin and to improve their educational standard in order to attain the status of choir monk,
and are disappointed if they fail to make the grade.
Brother Sylvester's brand of humility shows the mark of a
real vocation.

11

The Studies Director
and an American

BROTHER CHARLES

Walter Thomas Charles Hodgkinson was six feet tall, as thin as a lath and had the ascetic appearance of the ancient monk. He was the eldest son of a veterinary surgeon from the West Riding. The practice comprised his father and two partners, all expecting Walter to take over from his father.

Walter was sent to an expensive public school where he revelled in the academic side, but participated in as little sport as possible. His truly startling academic performance was crowned by a scholarship to Cambridge University.

Leaving school with the scholarship in his pocket, he secretly despised his native Yorkshire dialect. Trying to eliminate the Yorkshire short 'a' and substitute the Italian long 'a' in its place, he made a fool of himself by pronouncing the word 'gas' to rhyme with 'farce'. His family never let him forget it! As he matured, he often laughed at his early attempts and agreed that he had been a silly ass (pronounced with the Italian 'a').

At Cambridge, his progress was wholly academic. He came down with a first class B.A. degree in Classics and a research scholarship for his Ph.D. course.

His research subject was monastic history, which was surprising as his family were nominally Low Anglicans. This research brought him into contact with several monasteries, some, to his surprise, in the Anglican Communion, in which he became personally involved.

70

Considering becoming a monk, he talked to our abbot and novice master and was rather rebuffed when told that it was not a case of if he would like the life, but rather, had he the vocation from God. If he had, he would come eventually, if not, he would not stay if he came.

On showing persistence, he was advised to gain his Ph.D. first, then to come and stay in the guest-house for a time, where he would have to be instructed in the Catholic faith and make his first confession before entry as he was a Low Churchman. He would then be permitted to serve a six months' trial period or postulancy before entry as a novice. He decided to accept.

Thus it was that Walter Hodgkinson, B.A., Ph.D., came to the monastery. He knew as much about monastic history as the novice master and with regard to Latin and Greek, his degree stood him in good stead. Academically, he was miles ahead of the other entrants.

He got through to temporary vows feeling a bit frustrated, study wise, but he found in his last year before life profession that he was free to take up his studies where he had laid them down after his Ph.D. He was delighted to have finished with cooking and manual labour and to be free to study.

Under the direction of the then master of studies, a venerable monk of eighty-nine summers who was a scholar after his own heart, he found that he received every encouragement. Books which he needed, if not in the monastery library, were purchased for him. He was given help and encouragement with a book which he had in mind to write. At the moment, as I write this book, he already has six treatises to his credit with, as always, another in mind. He received all the credit for these books, which were published in his name, but of course, being a monk, he could not receive the money which came from them. This went to the monastery.

He found that in all, he was able to devote about six hours a day to his writing and studies, this, of course, being fitted into the structure of the monastic observance.

He told us an amusing anecdote about his final course at Cambridge. He was light in weight if tall and he used to

cox one of the trial eights. They were training and the crew
were putting up such a bad show that he stopped them
close to the bank and told them what he thought of their
efforts in very colourful boating language. Having exhausted his repertoire, he looked up, and there stood his
confessor, recently acquired as a result of his connections
with the monastery.

After life profession, he was sent on lecture tours and
the fees which he received went to the monastery. He also
studied for and passed, his General Ordination Certificate, and was ordained.

The jolt came when the Master of Studies died. After the
funeral, the abbot sent for Dom Charles and announced
that he wanted him to take over the job. Dom Charles did
not want this, but under his vow of obedience, he knew
that he had to accept it.

The next day, he moved into his old friend's cell, with its
large area of bookshelves and big imposing desk. The bed
tucked away in an alcove looked like an afterthought. He
went to the window and viewed the road leading to the
village. It was deserted, and a solitary cock pheasant from
the nearby woods, strutted down the road in its gay plum-
age. Its shape and colour were exquisite, and he marvelled
at this perfect specimen of nature.

Dom Charles thought of the first time he had visited this
cell. He had received help, encouragement and guidance
from his friend, but he was alone now, and would have to
direct others in their studies—the raw monk, who would
stumble through his Greek translation and other subjects
for his General Ordination Examination, the lay brothers
who would want advice on reading matter.

His reverie was cut short by a tap on his door—his first
'customer'—who was rapidly followed by a procession of
others.

He found there was no time for his own studies during
the normal study period, but he was now allowed to study
in place of manual work. Far from having a lazy life, he
worked harder than ever before.

Fortunately he was not expected to coach the novitiate
for this was done by the novice master. Not until the

juniors were in their third and last year in temporary vows and were attached to the senior common-room, did they come under Dom Charles for their studies.

The Master of Studies sets the educational tone of the monastery. A good one is shown by the number of books produced by the monks, and the scholastic attainment of the monastery generally.

BROTHER BARTHOLOMEW

Duke John Blundell Bochenski presented a peculiar and unusual case. He was an American and 'Duke' was a Christian name not a title. Duke first entered an Anglican Benedictine monastery in South California, near the border and the Mexican town of Santa Cruz. We presume that the community settled there during the American/ Mexican war, doing missionary and medical work in Mexico and scratched a living from the unwilling soil. Today they can be in civilization in hours.

Here Duke was life professed and ordained as Dom Bartholomew. The "seven-year itch" began to trouble him and he wished to be at the centre of the Anglican faith which he had embraced. After discussion with his abbot, he was still adamant.

An English community was approached, and they agreed to take him. He settled in and all seemed to be well, apart from his American hyperbole, and he was popular in the community. His fellow monks teased him when he bragged. They told him about the American and English sailors in a bar. The American bragged about the size of American battleships. The Englishman said nothing until they saw a British midget submarine, then he explained that they were evolved to go down into the soup cookers of the latest battleship, which was so huge that they could not stir the soup by any other means.

Dom Bartholomew took the hint and sportingly told the story of two Tommies who had just run after a bus and missed it. Two American soldiers enquired if that was the way they had run away from Dunkirk. The Tommies dropped their packs and taking hold of the Americans, they dumped them in a horse trough and enquired if that was how they had crawled out of Pearl Harbour.

Dom Bartholomew's stock rose in the community. He was now officially a member and made a full contribution both as a priest and at work. He persuaded the abbot to purchase tools and equipment and organized the maintenance of the three cars, farm tractor, rotor plough, motor mowers and light lorry belonging to the community, thus saving a lot of money. He was in the American idiom a 'go-getter'.

His hobby was photography and he obtained permission to bring his equipment from America and set up a dark room. In this way he made a lot of money for the community by selling photographs of the abbey and grounds and of groups of visitors and the processions at Corpus Christi and Easter. He was responsible for radio microphones being carried in these processions and for the sale of the cassette recordings made.

So much for American 'drive'.

When he had been at the abbey for five years, he was permitted to spend his 'rest' with relatives in America and this seemed to unsettle him. There were more grandiose schemes suggested by him, but the chapter felt that they had spent enough on his ideas.

Another year passed which was a rather troubled one for Dom Bartholomew. He petitioned the abbot for the six month's ex-claustration which can be sanctioned to enable a monk in difficulties to live and support himself outside the monastery to think things over.

He set up a photographic business in London, presumably from capital borrowed from his relatives. Instead of returning after the six months he moved to larger premises at an address unknown to the community. There was rumoured to be a woman involved in the case.

With hindsight, it was obvious that he had no real vocation. He could have waited for a year or so and obtained an honourable secularization from the Church, but regrettably, he chose this way.

In the Middle Ages, canon law and civil law were one and the same thing. After this time there came about the gradual separation of the two, which accelerated with the years until today they are quite apart. The monk is dealt with under canon law but his civil rights are protected by civil law. For example, within living memory, civil law allowed a man to marry his deceased wife's sister, whereas canon law did not. Thus by the same rule, according to civil law, a monk is free to marry if he deserts his monastery, but under canon law, he is not, unless properly dispensed from his vows and if not, he could be excommunicated.

12

A Frenchman and a Resignation

BROTHER DENYS
Marcel Paul Selvagion was a Frenchman, the son of a physician from St Omer in the Pas de Calais, Northern France. He was a rather surprising applicant, since he came from a Roman-Catholic family. He began to be critical of the Roman Church when his father, hoping eventually to see him graduate in medicine, sent him to study at the Sorbonne in Paris.

As is usual with a university education, it taught Marcel to think round everything with which he came into contact. He emerged with the idea that there was not sufficient freedom in the Roman Church and he saw the Anglo-Catholic Church as having exactly the same precepts, yet allowing greater freedom for the individual to think for himself. This is probably quite correct, yet I would not think it worthwhile to change from the faith of one's birth.

However, be that as it may, he corresponded with the abbot of an Anglican monastery, in order to investigate the Church. This was when he was just twenty-one and still at the Sorbonne. Accordingly, he was invited over to spend two weeks in the monastery guest-house, during his holidays. He spoke only 'schoolboy' English, but was made to feel at home since several of the brethren spoke fluent French.

When he expressed interest in joining the community, the abbot pointed out that there were difficulties, as an entrant would need to produce evidence of baptism and confirmation in the Anglican Church. Marcel said that this was why he had wanted to come, to join the Church of

76

England. The abbot replied, rather dryly, that there were less drastic ways of joining the Church than becoming a monk.

Marcel said that he had not explained himself very well, he thought he had a monastic vocation but, in the circumstances, he could not commit himself to one of the many French monasteries in the Roman Church.

He was warned that he was taking a drastic step in deserting the Church of his birth. His reply was that he was not deserting the Faith, but only the inflexible grip of Rome.

The case seemed a very complex one, and the Council of Religious were called in to advise. They said that whilst they would not condone any poaching from the Roman Church, if the individual demanded it, they would not prevent his transfer, provided that he received proper instruction for Anglican baptism and confirmation. It was debatable whether actual baptism was required, since he was already baptized in the Catholic faith and one cannot be baptized twice.

Having agreed to this, Marcel went home and promised to return to the guest-house in a month's time when he would receive the instruction and be accepted as a postulant.

He was a typical Frenchman and his quaint attempts at English in his early days, endeared him to the community. He insisted on speaking English, even in the presence of French-speaking monks and he very quickly became so proficient that it was only on rare occasions that his speech gave him away. He had a habit, peculiar in a Frenchman—a mania for physical exercise. He spent all his spare time running in the grounds and was always the first to join a party for swimming in the river, whenever possible, even in the coldest weather. He was a short stocky man, with an abundance of curly black hair and an abundance of energy to match. Most of the community were content with five hours of manual work daily but it was a pleasure to work with the energetic Frenchman who was always willing to take the heavier share of the work.

On one occasion, in the orchard, he made a mistake

when he started to prune the apple trees in the French fashion. The French always saw off all the bottom branches to allow free passage of grass-mowing equipment under them so they finish up with trees that are all top growth. We, having less area under cultivation, use the bottom branches for fruiting as well. He was on his second tree before he was spotted. There are still two trees in the orchard, pruned French fashion and known as "Dom Denys's trees".

He was very fond of animals and was ever ready to volunteer for extra work, feeding hens, ducks, pigs, goats, and the small herd of dairy cows which constituted the monastery 'farm'. Incidentally, Marcel was responsible for the suggestion that we keep a few geese. These are excellent for the table and, as he pointed out, they make excellent 'watch-dogs'. This was after one of the burglaries mentioned elsewhere in this narrative. They also give warning of one of the chief enemies of the chicken run—foxes. There were many foxes about, and when the snow came, their tracks were much in evidence. We had one incident which was very amusing to all, except the hen concerned.

This hen was sitting on her nest when the fox appeared. He tried to get at her through the wire but it was too securely fastened. We could see the marks of his scratching when we examined things afterwards. He then went round the back of the nesting boxes, and attacked the hen's rearquarters as she sat on the nest. He was able to reach far enough to chew off her tail feathers and bite her bottom. The hen squawked blue murder and raised the alarm, but she still sat stoically on her nest.

When help arrived, the fox promptly ran off into the woods. From that time the hen was christened "Henrietta" and her history was retailed to all visitors to the hen houses. When her rearquarters healed up, she was none the worse except that her tail feathers never grew again. Thus Henrietta enjoyed her notoriety, and she went on laying until it was her turn for the pot.

Marcel was eventually noviced and became Brother Denys, since St Denys is the patron saint of France.

Attaining temporary vows the time arrived for his first 'rest' outside the monastery. Not surprisingly, he asked if he could go home for his rest. The monastery paid his return air fare between London Airport and Orly Airport, Paris.

He returned full of the joys of spring as usual and entered enthusiastically into the monastic round. Life profession came and passed uneventfully, except for the appearance of a large contingent of his family and friends from France. They were very much impressed by our monastery and its general observance, and Marcel's father appeared somewhat mollified after his disappointment over his son leaving the Roman Church.

After life profession, Dom Denys took a great interest in the farm and vegetable gardens and he was eventually given charge of them. He spent much of his siesta time in the fields with the tractor, either mowing or hay-making. The fields around the monastery were kept as pasture for the few cows, or were used for growing hay as fodder for them.

The chapter discussed using these fields for growing cereals, but there was a plentiful supply of cheap straw from a nearby farm as bedding for the animals and hay was a better proposition.

The kitchen gardens kept the community in potatoes, root-crops, beans, peas and brassicas, with a surplus for sale. The food bill for the poultry was more than covered by the sale of surplus eggs. The pigs were fed from kitchen waste, boiled for swill. There were plenty of surplus apples, pears, plums and soft fruits for sale also.

On one occasion, Dom Denys was detailed to check the outer perimeter fencing. The adjacent road carried a lot of traffic and the fence was sometimes demolished and left by the driver, unreported. Small boys enlarged the damage, which often led to unorthodox incidents. Two young mothers once entered thus, and appeared in the chapel choir at vespers. They were politely escorted to the guest narthex by the guestmaster, with their prams and children. There were also raids on the property. Conifers, ornamental trees, Christmas trees and trees to produce larch poles were grown for sale in the shop. Thieves stole some ornamental trees one summer and cleared the total stock of Christmas trees one December. We were donating several Christmas trees to children's homes and had to tell them that there were none for them. Do people not realize that robbing Church property is sacrilege, or do they not care nowadays?

Besides farming and gardening, Dom Denys, being a Frenchman and used to the Roman habit of having plaster statues of the saints, was distressed when he found that the supply of statues of St Benedict from France, had dried up. He maintained that France had let us down, so a Frenchman must make amends.

It was his initiative which led us to buy the moulding material known as high-melt Vinyl. He made wooden formers and placed a statue of St Benedict in them, pouring the melted Vinyl around the statue. When cold, the thick mould was peeled from the statue, and replacing it in the former, plaster of Paris was poured into it, producing a facsimile of the statue. The mould was used many times. Dom Denys wrote to his father, who contacted a Polish acquaintance who specialized in polishing these statues. The Polish gentleman very kindly made his technique available to us, and we were able to produce statues as good as those we had received from France.

One of our monks was an artist who painted the more expensive versions of the statues for sale in the shop.

BROTHER MARK
Samuel Peter Shutler was the son of a textile manufacturer in Nottingham. He had one sister but no brothers. His father was a self-made man who had started out as a commercial traveller in textiles.

When the Second World War came, the father was newly married. He joined the Army and survived the war, being demobilized with the rank of lieutenant. On returning home, he found that his firm's premises had been demolished in the blitz and he was jobless. He used his war gratuity to buy a partnership in another struggling textile firm and they built up a reasonable business.

Soon he was able to buy out his partner. Business boomed and his son and daughter were born. The daughter went to university, but the son would not work for the necessary examinations, despite the expensive schooling he had received. He was more interested in the motorcycle which his doting father bought him.

After the inevitable crash, which led to an endorsed licence and landed him in hospital, his father bought him a sports car. He was in his element, rallying with the latest girlfriend beside him. He was a good-looking lad, tall slim and dark and the girls queued up to accompany him.

At eighteen, Samuel left school. He spent his evenings until the early hours attending the new disco clubs. His father obtained for him employment in the local government offices—considering he had no university degree, this was a good job. Here he settled as a junior clerk, undertaking to work at night school for the necessary examinations.

Samuel was soon in trouble at work, due to bad attendance. His father managed to extricate him from his difficulties on the grounds of ill health, with the connivance of a medical friend. Samuel mournfully reconciled himself to a compulsory curtailment of liberty.

The family attended the local Anglo-Catholic Church. There was a girl in the congregation in whom Samuel was interested and he volunteered as a thurifer to impress her.

When Samuel became due for a holiday, his father insisted on his spending part of it at a monastery for a retreat. To make sure that Samuel arrived there, his father delivered him personally in the family Daimler.

The boy lapped up the idea of being waited upon as a guest in the monastery. He exuded his natural charm and sought interviews with the senior officers of the monastery. They were suitably impressed by the charming lad who left behind a good impression, and a donation of one hundred pounds to the community funds.

Afterwards, Samuel was unusually silent and his parents thought that the retreat had done him good. Actually he was debating the possibility of exchanging his job for what he thought would be an easy life in the monastery. He realized the restrictions and that women had no part of the monastic life. Could he not get out at night however, as he had done from the paternal home? After another *mauvais quart d'heure* with his boss at work, Samuel decided to try the monastery and handed in his notice immediately. He was promptly told that he could leave immediately without working his notice.

The next day, he motored over to the monastery and made formal application. He was accepted in principle and sent home to wind up his affairs.

The day of entry came. He went with his father's blessing and arrived at the monastery with an escort of girls and lads of his own age. They arrived in two-seater sports cars with hooting horns and revving engines. The scandalized guestmaster went out to see what the noise was, anticipating an invasion of 'Hell's Angels' as had happened previously.

Explanations forthcoming, Samuel was conducted to the novice master and his friends given tea in the guesthouse. Samuel expected to donate his car to the monastery for the use of the occupants—himself included. This being refused, it was driven back by a passenger from another car.

Samuel passed the required medical. Despite former dissipation, he was a perfect physical specimen.

Over the next six months he began to wonder if he had in fact, to quote his own words "backed a loser". However, his natural charm helped him secure the relatively easy sacristy jobs; laying out vestments and cleaning altar plate were vastly preferable to laying concrete and gardening. Because of his home Church experience, he found favour with the sacristan, and was started as an acolyte long before others.

There was one humorous incident. He noticed that there was a sink in the sacristy, the drain of which led into the ground instead of into the drain. On enquiry, the sacristan explained, "That, my lad, is a piscina and the first one that does will be shot by me, personally!" Actually this is for pouring holy water away, which, having been blessed, is not mixed with sewage. The name comes from the Roman fishpond, used for this purpose by early Christians.

Samuel soon evolved a scheme to exceed his one weekly letter. He obtained illicit stamps and posted the extra letters during the Sunday afternoon compulsory walk. He also cultivated the habit of nipping into the village after 'lights out', dressed in 'civvies'—each postulant kept his secular clothes in his cell, in case he left the monastery. He was not tonsured as a postulant, so his haircut was not remarkable. He placed a short ladder from the workshop to the sacristy roof and got in through a senior cell window, which was always open at night. Samuel nearly got caught when the senior heard him and called, "Who is there?" Samuel crouched in the shadows until the senior left the cell and, spotting the ladder, went down to investigate. Samuel nipped through the cell and back to his own cell. At the inevitable enquiry, it was assumed that the intruder had fled when challenged. The police took no action other than to warn their cars to keep a lookout. The workshop staff were rebuked for not locking up the ladder. They were certain that they had locked it up. Little did they know that Samuel possessed a duplicate key.

Thus Samuel misspent his postulancy. His charm however secured admission to the novitiate. After novicing he had the monastic tonsure and this made nocturnal excursions difficult, as the tonsure was very noticeable. He tried one excursion, proposing to wear a hat and this was his downfall. He returned to the monastery about 3.00 a.m. and saw several lights on. He skirted round to his ladder and was shocked to find it missing.

It appears that a monk had occasion to go to the workshop, as he had left a light on. Swinging his torch, he spotted the ladder and raised the alarm. The ladder was locked up and the grounds searched. Samuel, arriving at this point, realized what was happening, also that a novice would not be called out for this. Furthermore, he was dressed in 'civvies'. He tried to gain the door, but was spotted by one of the monks who gave chase and brought him down with a perfect rugby tackle.

The game was up! Explanations being unsatisfactory, Samuel was confined to his cell pending enquiries. The story came out and Samuel asked to be released from the novitiate, rather than wait to be sent away.

The mystery is how he managed to get this far. No one has ever tried to go on nocturnal excursions before, to my knowledge, nor has anyone since. Where he went he refused to say.

He was fetched away by his sister, and we heard that he did not return home. Personally, I would not be surprised to hear that he came to a sticky end.

He had some good ideas, one of which was the introduction of a games room, with billiards and table tennis. Rather unmonastic, but appreciated by the younger monks. It mystified me how a novice was able to get this idea put forward.

13

Epidemic!

When an epidemic breaks out under normal circumstances outside a monastery, repercussions can arise, with
contacts spreading the infection to most unlikely places.
When it arises within the confines of a monastery, there is
little chance of any of the inhabitants avoiding succumb-
ing to it. This is why an infirmarian and helpers are
appointed, to detect the cases of infection and, it is hoped,
confine the infection to as few contacts as possible. However, when the infection is serious, the damage is done
before the isolation routine can be put into practice. The
contacts are then incubating the disease before the first
victim becomes ill and unless one is immune, one cannot
avoid getting the infection.

Such was the case in the last Asian 'flu epidemic. One of
the brethren who had been attending the hospital as an
out-patient, brought news of the spreading epidemic. We
think it was introduced to us by a guest who came with
obvious symptoms. The day after entry, his condition
worsened. His retreat was abandoned and the infirmarian
saw him and prescribed bed, hot-water bottles and a liquid
diet. The next day, the doctor was called; he diagnosed
Asian 'flu and left instructions to continue the infirmarian's treatment, with a prescription for tablets.

The workshop squad put in a bell for the patient to
summon help between the infirmarian's four-hourly visits
to administer the tablets. There is no infirmary as such in
a Benedictine monastery, and the sick are tended in their
own rooms. In this case, hot soup and cold drinks were
supplied in thermos flasks from the kitchens.

The organization was getting into its stride when two

85

more cases were diagnosed, another guest and the retreat director of the first one. After this more casualties appeared daily with the result that the infirmary staff had to be augmented. With so many sick, the work list could not be adhered to and only essentials were kept going.

One guest left, against the doctor's advice, since he was trying to contain the epidemic. Soon the situation became serious, with one half of the community nursing the other. I had thought I was immune, but one morning I awoke with nausea and dizziness and by evening I was really groggy. I tried to keep on my feet to help out but retired gratefully after compline and was thankful that it was my morning in next day. Each monk gets a morning in weekly, which means that he is not required for the night office at 5.00 a.m., but he can sleep until 7.00 a.m., attending prime after breakfast. This is necessary with a working day from 5.00 a.m. until 10.00 p.m.

When my alarm went off at 7.00 a.m. I tried to get out of bed, struggled to my feet and promptly sat down again as my legs gave way. I felt weak, sick and very hot and dizzy. When I did not appear, the infirmarian checked up on me and brought me some hot, sweet coffee and ladylike fingers of buttered toast. Toast is a delicacy which only the sick receive and we often say that we only get toast when we are too ill to eat it.

When the infirmarian collected the tray, I lay, alternately perspiring and shivering, and trying to say my office. He took the book away and said the abbot would dispense me from saying it.

I just lay, sweating it out. Frequently someone appeared with the command, "Drink this." I drank but I have no notion what it was. I have a vague recollection of someone turning back the bed-clothes and running a stethoscope over my back and chest—probably the doctor.

When I opened my eyes it was broad daylight, but I quickly shut them again as the pain was blinding. I relaxed and let the pain ride.

I must have slept. The door opened and a boisterous voice said, "Wakey wakey. Everything stops for tea." A tray was deposited by the bed, containing the inevitable toast fingers and tea. "Cheerio. Enjoy yourself," said the voice and he was gone. The top of my head rose at every remark and settled as the door closed. I had a raging thirst which the tea eased and I managed a bite of toast.

That night I slept little. My back ached, my head ached and I sweated abominably. The next day passed similarly, except that once the door burst open and a clean sheet and pillow slip landed on the bed, closely followed by a towel. My grunt must have alerted the lay brother that I was in bed, because he remarked, "Sorry! Didn't know you had got it as well." The door banged. Despite years in the monastery, this brother always banged doors.

Slowly I returned to the land of the living, to be told that most of the community were suffering from the 'flu. I wanted to help, but the infirmarian was adamant since one of the brethren was already fighting pneumonia resulting from getting up too soon.

I was told that the third 'wave' were now going down but the first wave were up again and helping. Miraculously the infirmarian seemed to be immune. All were helping with trays for the sick if not in bed.

At last I was allowed up, provided I had a few mornings in. I was glad to help. The District Nurse, christened "Sweety Pie" by the community, joined in the fray, escorted by the abbot. The doctor himself succumbed and a lady doctor took his place, also escorted. One of the elderly monks tucked the bed-clothes under his chin and said, "Go away. I'm not having a woman in here." The abbot remonstrated with him and he submitted reluctantly.

The hospital was overcrowded, so the doctor left our patients in our care unless complications set in. One of the guests had to be removed and he died in hospital which dampened our spirits. The situation was not improved when one of the monks, in bed with a heart attack, also contracted the virus. His heart was unable to stand the strain and he died. The brethren prepared him for burial and the undertaker was summoned. The monk's relatives were warned of the danger of infection, but they still attended his funeral. Only about six monks and the abbot were available. They conducted the service, prepared food for the relatives and dug the grave.

The abbot was literally 'out on his feet' at the funeral and the following day he was confined to bed. The rest struggled on and it is to their eternal credit that no one asked for a drink or a bed-pan in vain.

By this time the sick had been gathered in the senior common-room to ease the load on the helpers and at one time there were about fifty beds there. The car drivers succumbed and we were virtually cut off, but the village store rallied round and delivered necessities.

The helpers had no time to prepare their food so they existed on sandwiches. The abbot seemed to be made of granite. He recovered the quickest and was soon on duty dispensing soups and drinks and emptying bed-pans. He also took the sacrament round.

The District Nurse did not become ill—apparently she had been inoculated. She spent all her time at the monastery and at last the turning point was reached. More helpers arose from bed to give the last five or so a chance to sleep.

As the situation improved, the community gathered in the kitchen for meals. Soon the numbers grew and the refectory was cleared for use again. When there were sufficient, they started the recitation of the office in chapel again and Mass was again celebrated.

The few remaining sick were wrapped in blankets and taken to their cells. The chief problem was the housework. The kitchen was a shambles and the ovens and gas rings needed cleaning. The floor needed scrubbing, and supplies, hurriedly dumped on the floor, needed putting away. The corridors, usually mopped daily and oiled every second day, were covered in dust. The refectory tables needed scrubbing, and the floor polishing. The guest-house was derelict and it needed thoroughly cleaning before re-occupation. The senior common-room was a shambles. Spare beds were still standing in it and piles of dirty sheets awaited removal and washing. The laundry was re-started with augmented staff. It is amazing how much washing accumulates for fifty or sixty people when left for a few days.

The monastery awoke from its lethargy, shook itself and took stock—two dead, one a visitor whom we mourned, but not with the same personal loss as our brother who had succumbed. Otherwise, there were no permanent scars. Our prayers for the dead, the dying and the sick in body, mind and spirit had lapsed. On the mundane side, the guest quarters had been closed. The workshops had closed. We had nothing to sell in the shop, even if there had been customers.

Visitors started to arrive again. The workshop started up. A cross was made and engraved for the grave of our dead brother, ready for erection. The events of the last three weeks faded like a bad dream.

14

Brother Leo

Albert Edward Dunworth is a Cornishman, although his name does not sound like it. He is a very placid, quietly spoken individual with an accent unmistakably Cornish in origin.

He presented himself at the monastery immediately after the Second World War, during which he had been a conscientious objector. He never talked about that phase of his life, although no doubt this information had been imparted to the abbot on joining. He had received an ordinary state school education, supplemented by night school and extra-mural studies of his own seeking. He was very intelligent, and would probably have managed to become a choir monk by hard study, but he preferred to serve as a lay brother.

His early childhood was spent in the seaside resort of Falmouth, in his native Cornwall. His father was a fisherman and owned his own boat, in which he spent many nights at sea in the fishing season, standing out beyond Pendennis Head, or further into Falmouth Bay when the seas ran higher. The elder son helped in the fishing business.

Albert's mother let her sitting-room and front bedroom in the summer when visitors arrived. If the visitors had children who were too old to sleep in their parent's room, the second bedroom was pressed into service and the family managed with camp-beds in the kitchen. The younger sister occupied the third bedroom, vacating it to stay with a nearby aunt when paying guests needed it.

The family were used to this 'general post' during the holiday season, and accepted it without question. After all, one had to make money whilst it was available.

Young Albert was happy enough. Much of his summer holidays was spent in and out of the sea with his friends and he could swim like a fish. After he left school, he made up his mind that fishing was not for him. He had been out with his father and brother on a few occasions, and he was not at all keen on the life. He drifted into one of the only two occupations of the district—that of coach driving in the summer, and serving in one of the shops in winter. Failing a job in a shop in the winter, it was a case of going on the dole.

Wages, during the season, were high in the coach industry, and he gained a lot in tips. When war came he received very harsh treatment from the authorities as he stood by his convictions and refused to do military service. There are various schools of thought regarding conscientious objectors, but knowing the man I would say his convictions were genuine, even if I feel that he was misguided.

After the war Albert went back to the coach company. They kept their best men on during the winter and Albert was kept on when others were not. It was during one of these off-season outings that Albert took a party from his church to visit the monastery. He was a regular church attender and a church worker so he joined the party of men who were conducted round the abbey, and was very intrigued with it all.

He took the first opportunity of making a retreat at the monastery, and as one thing led to another, he offered himself as a postulant to the lay brotherhood, and was accepted.

He passed through his postulancy, novitiate, and into life vows without incident and at the time that we meet him in the monastery, he has been life professed for fifteen years and has held the post of guestmaster for several years. As he was used to being a 'loner', the solitary life of the monk was no hardship to him.

His accommodation was austere but fairly comfortable, in fact better than he had been used to during the periods of 'general post' at home. Being in life vows the strict austerity of his monastic cell had been relaxed somewhat.

Our lay Brother Leo found himself in charge of a little domain of his own, with another brother in temporary vows to assist him. Whilst everything went well, and there were no complaints from guests, Brother Leo was left to his own devices. He was an intelligent man and very soon cultivated an intelligent approach to others, emulating some of the guests and choir monks. Many visitors addressed him as "Dom Leo" thinking that he was a choir monk. This mistake he quickly corrected, thus showing his humility, which is an essential attribute of a monk.

The guest-house was made up of a new building and the altered stables of the original stately home in which the monastery was housed. The monks had rebuilt and added to the original stable buildings when the guest-house was opened.

Many religious communities take over stately homes, which are sometimes offered to them by the owners. They are then altered by the monks to suit monastic requirements. This is a less expensive process than building from scratch, but there are disadvantages, in that there is often an order designating them as buildings of architectural interest so that there are restrictions on external alterations.

The guest-house contained about twenty single rooms, fairly comfortably furnished with furniture derived from oblates and friends and from monks who had entered life vows and disposed of their possessions. According to the Rule of St Benedict, the guestmaster must keep all the rooms in the guest-house ready for occupation at all times, with rooms aired and beds made up. Guests are expected to make their own beds whilst in occupation and they are provided with a room key. The locking of doors was found necessary because all kinds of people come to the guest-house. Genuine people are in the vast majority—they come for a retreat, make it faithfully and depart, leaving a donation to the community to cover their board and keep. No one is ever asked for a donation, but it is expected that guests will contribute according to their means.

Without listing names, I would like to give some idea of the antics which some guests get up to.

I mentioned alcoholics and drug addicts earlier but the monastery has to contend with petty theft also. On one occasion the workshop was broken into and stripped of all the portable tools and power tools. The police were unable to discover very much, and the culprits avoided capture. There were signs of a lorry having stood in the lane outside the wall and marks on the wall indicated that heavy items had been passed over it. There was one really beautiful example of a thumb-print on the outer door of the workshop. On enquiry, it was found that Scotland Yard had no record of this on their files and by a process of elimination it was found that it belonged to one of the workshop staff.

The police came to the conclusion that the workshop had been 'cased' by somebody staying in the guest-house who had obtained a soap impression of the key. This was an easy matter since the key was usually left in the door when the workshop was open. It was then remembered that two strangers had stayed in the guest-house just prior to the theft and the monk in charge of the workshop could remember them trying to obtain admittance to the workshops which was forbidden to guests. One actually entered the workshops to talk to him, whilst his pal stood outside the door—an admirable opportunity for him to whip out the key and take a soap impression. The police laboratory said that there were in fact traces of soap left on the key, even though it had been used for some time afterwards. Half-remembered descriptions of the pair could have fitted anyone.

On another occasion, after strangers had stayed in the guest-house, the door of the sacristy was forced during the night and gold and silver plate was stolen. This included a gold and silver medieval chalice presented to the community on the occasion of the visit of a Spanish abbot and some of his monks. Again, nothing was ever traced. The police said that the gold and silver ware would be on the night boat to Rotterdam before the theft was discovered and, the following morning, any easily recognized item would be melted down.

Not only the every-day altar plate but also the ceremonial plate, which was very valuable and had been donated over many years, had been stolen. In addition, the altars had been stripped of the sacred vessels laid out for the following morning's early Mass.

We were not the only people who suffered, for several large houses and farms in the neighbourhood were also burgled. In one case, a householder heard a noise in the garden one night and looking out of the bedroom window he saw a man carrying his motor-mower out of his shed. The householder had an air-gun and pellets in his wardrobe, and loading it, took several pot-shots at the posterior of the man as he bent over the mower. Letting out a loud howl the intruder bolted over the fence. When the householder reported this to the police, they were unable to find the thief but they prosecuted the householder for causing grievous bodily harm to a person unknown. He was fined five pounds when the case came before the magistrates.

Thieves today, stoop to robbing the House of God, when years ago they would have drawn the line at this. I am tempted to ask what kind of man would actually strip the altars?

The community of course carried insurance and was reimbursed financially, but nothing could replace the plate acquired over the years for each piece had a history.

We have digressed somewhat and to return to the duties of the guestmaster—he also had to contend with petty thefts from the guest-house—cushions, blankets and even small items of furniture vanished.

Another part of the guestmaster's territory was the guest reception area, comprising a lounge, dining-rooms and shop, as well as small parlours, where guests could be interviewed. The shop was the responsibility of other monks but the area generally was always open to the public and was at first left unattended when the community was in chapel singing the office. It later became necessary to have an intern oblate on duty because of thefts of books and handicrafts from this area.

A monastery is not even immune from vandalism. The guestmaster reported cases where a guest-house room had been wrecked by departing guests.

A particular guest arrived without warning and asked

for the abbot. He was told that he was not available without an appointment so he settled for talking with the guestmaster. He said that he had come to join the community but he was told that this was not possible without a long period of probation. Interviews with the abbot and novice master were necessary and the background of the applicant must be probed. Then a long period elapsed whilst the applicant lived in the monastery before being admitted for life.

On being told this, the applicant asked if he could stay in the guest-house. Two days later the abbot saw him and reiterated what the guestmaster had told him. However, as he was so keen, perhaps he would return home and come back in a month's time, when his background had been investigated? The would-be entrant then confessed that he had given up his lodgings and his job when he came to the monastery with the result that he had nowhere to go. Could he stay in the monastery while he looked for a job? He said he would reimburse the monastery when he found one.

In the meantime, he had a series of mysterious accidents. He had a fall in his room, tripping over and breaking a chair leg which was then mended in the workshop and he fell up the steps of the guest reception, in both cases sustaining cuts and bruises. When he tripped over the step on the pathway leading up to the guest-house one night, the abbot thought that something should be done about his injuries. There was lighting between the main buildings and the guest-house so the step was well lit. However, the step was taken out by the workshop, and replaced by a concrete ramp.

The abbot saw him about his injuries and said he wanted him to go to the out-patient department of the local hospital as he had a nasty head injury. Despite his protests (understandable in the light of subsequent events) the abbot arranged for the monastery car to take him to the hospital, accompanied by a monk. The monk and guest were both waiting in the casualty reception when the would-be entrant suddenly fell forward out of his chair in what was obviously an epileptic fit. The question of the mysterious falls was solved.

After attention at the hospital, they returned to the monastery and the monk reported the incident to the abbot, who sent for the man and asked why he had concealed his condition. The would-be entrant said he had kept it quiet because he had obtained a job in the nearby town as a machine operator to start the following Monday. He had actually given the abbot's name as a reference.

The abbot said he could not let him go amongst machinery in his condition and the employer must be told. Despite his pleas, the abbot picked up the telephone and spoke to the employer, who said he certainly could not offer this type of job to an epileptic.

Our friend then raved at the abbot and accused him of stopping him from finding employment. The abbot said he was prepared to help him in spite of this and that he could stay in the guest-house while the possibilities of getting him a job were explored but he insisted that any prospective employer must be informed of his condition. At the same time it was pointed out the epilepsy was a definite bar to entering the monastery as he would fail the rigorous medical examination required.

The would-be entrant became very angry and was abominably rude to the abbot, whose reply was that in that case, there was nothing more that could be done for him and he would be sent away. As he had no money the abbot provided him with some pocket-money and the necessary rail tickets home and sent him to the station in the monastery car, with instructions to the driver to see that he left on the London train. The unpleasant surprise came after he had left. The guestmaster found that his room had been vandalized, furniture, mirrors and windows having been broken.

The guestmaster brought to light another case where the monastery was considerably the poorer.

An American visitor arrived and said that he was temporarily without funds and was waiting for a sum of money to be 'wired' from the States, could he stay with us for a few days until it arrived, when he would make a "generous donation" to the funds?

It was explained to him that under our Rule, any traveller could seek accommodation with us and there was no fixed charge, but travellers paid what they could afford. He was housed in the guest-house and fed in the refectory with the other guests.

One evening, a few days later, he asked the guestmaster if he could make a local telephone call. The guestmaster took him inside the enclosure and found a suitable extension for him in a quiet corner. There were several extensions inside the enclosure, but no telephone outside where the guests were accommodated. A coin-operated 'pay phone' has since been fitted in guest reception for the use of guests.

The guestmaster then left him in order to attend to another guest but was amazed to find him replacing the receiver over half an hour later. The American explained that he had only just managed to get through and that he would pay for the call when his money arrived. The next day he departed for London, saying that he would return that evening, taking with him the large brief-case which was the only luggage with which he arrived.

He never returned but when the next telephone bill arrived, there was one item, a transatlantic telephone call that cost about fifty-eight pounds. There is no prize for guessing who made the call.

On another occasion, the guestmaster used his pass-key to enter the room of a guest, who had gone out for the day and left his electric light on. He noticed that there were several new books in the room, which had obviously come from our bookshop, and he thought that the guest had borrowed them to read. There is a library for the use of guests and the guestmaster made a mental note to tell the guest that it was not permitted to take new books from the bookshop to read unless they were paid for. These books were worth over twenty pounds.

When the guest returned and the guestmaster spoke to him, he said that he had paid for the books. The guestmaster knew this was not so, as he would have taken the money for them himself. The guest explained that as there had been nobody there he had put the money in one of the donation boxes. The guestmaster left him in order to place the money in the correct account. He found that there was nothing like this amount of money in any of the boxes and after enquiring if anyone had emptied the boxes, he reported the matter to the abbot.

The abbot saw the guest in his office and suggested that if he cared to correct the 'oversight' the matter could be closed. The guest insisted that he had paid for them and that someone had emptied the box, whereupon the abbot said that the police would be making one of their routine visits the following day and it would be a good idea if the guest had departed when they arrived.

The guest departed and took the books with him. Furthermore, he left no donation to cover his ten-day stay.

The guestmaster also told this amusing story. When the outer doorbell of the monastery rings, one never knows what one will find on the other side. The guestmaster answered the door one day to find a young couple outside. The young man asked "Do you marry here?" The guestmaster thought that he was enquiring about the monastic life and replied that all the orders which he knew were celibate. It turned out that the couple thought that it would be good gimmick to be married in a monastery—needless to say they were disappointed. They then pressed their luck by enquiring about the "block of flats" currently being built in the monastery grounds and asked if there were any to let. This was a new extension to the guesthouse which we were building.

When the doorbell rang on another occasion, there stood a farmer with a lorry-load of potatoes. He said he had just delivered a load to the "Ladies' department" up the road and they had suggested that we might be interested. We had never heard the local Roman Catholic convent referred to like this before.

On another occasion one of the guests heard the sound of conversation in the next guestroom during the night. On enquiry, he found that there was a rather queer character there who had a statue of St Francis with him; when he could not sleep he would talk to the statue. Later, a friend arrived and was put in the room on the other side of the queer character and warned what to expect. That night the first visitor was awoken by a scuffling sound and thinking that the pantomime was starting, he put on his light only to see a little fieldmouse sitting in his fireplace. This was before central heating was put in the guest-house and rooms were furnished with open fires and fire-irons.

The mouse sat still when he 'shushed' at it and he reached for a shoe and threw it at it. The shoe landed amongst the fire-irons with a clatter and the mouse vanished. When asked, the following morning, if he had slept well the friend exploded, "The silly fool next door didn't talk, but I heard him 'shushing' away to himself, the next moment I thought murder was being done from the infernal clatter!"

15

Nibblers

Apart from prospective entrants into the monastery, there are a number of people who apply for admission who have no hope of being accepted for the postulancy or even as intern oblates; the abbot calls them "nibblers".

Whilst it is open to anyone to become an extern oblate of any religious house, before acceptance for residence within the monastery certain conditions must be fulfilled. To become an intern oblate it is necessary to make some sort of contribution towards one's own support. Special arrangements are sometimes made in special cases, for example, extern oblates who have met with personal problems or have become ill, are sometimes accepted as intern oblates. Anyone applying for admission as a monk, must become a postulant.

Some applicants are intrigued by the novelty of the life; some want to get away from a problem in the outside world, as for example, being dissatisfied with their job, some want to come to what they fondly imagine will be an easy life—these only see the monks chanting the office in choir and they think that is all there is to the life. Some come because they want to give their lives to God and are willing to sacrifice everything to this end. The latter is the only true foundation for building a monastic vocation.

The variety of people who try to enter a monastery is amazing. In one case on record, a man of about thirty years of age, with a black eye, presented himself. It appeared that there had been an argument with his wife and he wanted to enter the monastery where she could not reach him. All that could be done was to pass him on to a com-

munity of nursing sisters who would give him a home until
his affairs could be sorted out.

On another occasion, a young man applied, beating the
police squad-car by only a short head. He was being interviewed by the abbot when the police arrived. How they
knew where to find him is a mystery, one can only hope
that it was not due to the reputation of the monastery. As
one of the 'wayfarers' was heard to remark, "You can't
trust these monks!"

One man said quite openly that he had just been
diagnosed as having inoperable cancer. He had heard that
a similar case had once been received by the monastery
and he seemed to think that a precedent had been created.
It was explained that this had been a special case and that
the man in question was an extern oblate with no surviv-
ing relatives. It was a matter of "looking after our own"
and we had neither room nor equipment nor staff to deal
with more than one case of this nature. We recommended a
nursing order of nuns and said we were prepared to pray
for him and visit him if he wished it.

On several occasions, relatives wanted us to take an
aged father who was "cramping their style". In fact, in the
Middle Ages, elderly people often retired into a monastery
to end their days.

Often potential entrants would present themselves
whilst suffering from some disease, as in the case of the
epileptic previously mentioned. This complaint they proposed to keep quiet about. The poor souls did not realize
that they would be given a rigorous medical examination,
and that the doctor would have to certify that they were
capable of performing the very strenuous work which they
would have to do, particularly in their early years at the
monastery.

The case that really took us aback, was that of a young
woman, obviously of the breed of 'Women's Libbers' who
are the granddaughters and great granddaughters of
Mrs Pankhurst's Suffragettes. She roared up to the
monastery one morning in her own little Triumph Spitfire
sports car, and pounded the doorbell as if it were a fire
alarm. When the doorkeeper answered, she demanded (I

mean demanded, not asked for) an interview with the abbot and the doorkeeper took her to him. Arriving at the abbot's door, the monk knocked, but the young woman brushed past rudely, and flinging open the door, demanded to know whether she was speaking to the abbot. When the surprised abbot admitted that she was correct in her assumption, she demanded to be received as a postulant on the grounds of sexual equality.

The abbot was rather taken aback, but, not showing it in any way, he suggested that she wanted the convent down the road. She became very abusive and the situation deteriorated to the point where the police had to be called to put her out. It was evidently a "Women's Lib" stunt to exert her right of entry into a man's domain.

Such people are, of course, quite mad. Any woman worthy of her salt can demonstrate her superiority over the mere male by exerting her womanly wiles to gain her own way. In trying to compete in the same arena with men on equal terms she is treated as another man, and the battle is lost for her before it commences.

Countless men present themselves at the monastery, after going through some personal traumatic experience, such as losing their wife, either by death or other circumstances. This is not a good basis for starting life as a monk and usually, the delaying tactics of the Church prevent them from doing anything foolish. Unless there were other reasons apart from this for their entry, it is unlikely that they would be allowed to enter the monastery until at least two years had elapsed.

Many presenting themselves are mere youngsters fresh from school. Others imagine that the life is easy—they never see the monastery at five o'clock on a winter's morning with the temperature several degrees below freezing-point and deep snow to be shovelled away before the animals in the sheds can be reached to be fed and watered. Nor do they see the kitchens on a summer day, with the kitchen staff sweating to turn out about sixty dinners in a temperature of well over a hundred degrees when the big ovens are working. They can never know the feeling of aridity which the monk can experience when the comfort of prayer vanishes, the feeling of desolation which one feels when it seems that one is deserted by both God and man. All these things the monk will take in his stride if he has a true vocation.

The question of discernment of vocation is a complex one. Generally, neither the aspirant nor anyone else, no matter how experienced, can discern on the spot whether he has a vocation although it is easier to spot lack of vocation. A so-called vocation is often wrapped up in the wishes and desires of the aspirant and it is impossible to tell whether it is a true one or not. Only the passage of time can prove this.

The fact that he has applied for entry to the monastery may be a prompting from God, or it may be that the imagined 'glamour' of the monastic life has influenced him. If the urge does in fact come from God, the aspirant would be very wrong to ignore it. This is why such a long time is taken in the so-called 'testing' of one's vocation.

If a man becomes a monk, he must exchange all for a life of solitude, for long hours of hard work without any reward save that of knowing that he is closer to God. He must be prepared for spiritual dryness, for desolation when once the initial glow has faded, for boredom even and sometimes for intense frustration.

If a man is prepared for all this, he is best advised to try his vocation. If he decides to take this course, the question arises as to which order he should join. He has the choice of several 'open' orders, such as those whose main work is in the mission field, or an 'enclosed' order, of which the Benedictine Order is an example of the more moderate and the Cistercian (or Trappist) Order an example of the stricter observance.

It is advisable, however, to finish any course of study, as for example for a degree, before entering. Thus one has a career to fall back upon if unsuited to monastic life.

The aspirant will never know what life in a monastery is really like until he has tried it. All my own preconceived ideas were completely erroneous. This is why the emphasis is on the aspirant *trying* his vocation for he will never know unless he does see the life from the inside, neither will anyone else. In my case I left as a result of extreme internal reform in the Church in general and in the monastery in particular.

No matter how far one has gone into one's profession, there is no disgrace in coming away from the monastery, provided that one abides by the rules for leaving as laid down by the Church. There is no such thing today as being irrevocably committed for life. If one enters honestly with the genuine intention of fulfilling one's vows, the Church will grant an honourable dispensation if matters become intolerable.

After entry, it is necessary to serve six months as a postulant and during this period the bulk of the 'non-vocations' leave. The novice master then recommends one for the year's novitiate at his discretion. There follows three years in temporary vows, dependent upon one obtaining the necessary two-thirds majority of chapter votes. One is then considered for life profession if one gets the same two-thirds majority of chapter votes and passes the interview with the abbot and the various bishops connected with the monastery.

One remains a 'Brother' and can still be dispensed from vows by the abbot, until life profession, when one becomes a 'Dom' if a choir monk. At this stage, one can only be dispensed in the Anglo-Catholic Church, by the Archbishop of Canterbury, on the advice of the interested bishops.

Only about one in five or six postulants will eventually attain life profession.

If a member of another faith wishes to enter, then it is of course, necessary for him to embrace the Christian faith of the denomination of the monastery which he wishes to enter. This sometimes happens, and the person is given instruction, baptism and confirmation before entry. Having once been received, they must demonstrate that they are prepared to be a practising Christian, otherwise they would be asked to resign or be sent away.

16

A Welshman and Two Irishmen

BROTHER DAVID

Gwillym Lloyd Roberts was a Welshman. He was very small being only just five feet tall in his socks and extremely sensitive about it. He came to us, at his own request, from a Dominican foundation in South Wales, at the age of twenty.

His home was in North Wales and he came from the village of Llangernyw, not far from Llanrwst. He was the son of a local butcher and had received a good education at a boarding school. He had the necessary examination passes to gain entrance to university but decided to throw it all over to enter the Dominican foundation. He kept quiet about the university entrance as he knew that the Dominicans would have sent him back to complete the course if they had known.

The Dominicans are an open order—a preaching order of friars. This did not appeal to our friend as his somewhat pompous bearing in a man of his size, made him look ridiculous.

After completing his novitiate, he was convinced that he had a monastic vocation but he wanted to move to a contemplative order so it was decided to let him try his vocation in a Benedictine foundation. Having been in a monastery before, he thought that he knew all about the monastic life. What he did not realize was that an enclosed order is very different from an open one.

He arrived with the idea, apparently, of teaching us how to run the monastery. He was not pleased when the novice master insisted upon his starting again as a postulant. He thought that having once served a year as a novice, he should be allowed to proceed to temporary vows. He often argued that he was being victimized and given a rough time by the novice master. This was not so. The fact was that he had a flair for getting himself noticed when he did anything wrong. His small stature ensured that he could be spotted amongst a group of novices, from half a mile away. His observance was good, he knew the 'drill' and he knew the liturgy, but he was always being reprimanded for breaking the rule of silence. Coming from an open order where freer speech was allowed, he was often tempted to open his mouth when he should have kept it shut.

His initiation in manual labour was uneventful, except that he strongly resented it when a big, beefy lad tried to help him with a heavy job. It was rather amusing to see the little fellow with flashing eyes, putting a big, six foot, fifteen stone, nineteen-year-old in his place. He reminded one of a bad-tempered bantam cock. When on the compulsory Sunday afternoon walks, the others used to tease him by taking long strides and walking fast, to see him try to keep in step with a hop, skip and jump.

On one occasion the party was crossing the fields when one youngster, who was country bred, said there was an 'old tup' or male sheep loose in the field and he strongly advised walking round. The little Welshman was quite certain that he was wrong. He set off across the field and the others followed cautiously, keeping an eye on a possible escape route.

Our friend 'Taffy' was about half way across, when the animal pawed the ground. 'Taffy' realized that something was wrong and started to make a quick retreat. The animal began to trot towards him and Taffy broke into a run. The rest of the party made for the nearest fence and retreated over it. 'Taffy' hoisted up the skirts of his cassock and made an attempt on the two-hundred yards sprint record, his bare legs twinkling in the summer sunlight, with the animal in close pursuit. He made the fence a good yard ahead of the animal and was hoisted over it, somewhat ignominiously, by the rest of the party. The animal braked suddenly and stood snorting.

Afterwards, one only had to refer to the incident in

'Taffy's' presence to make him gnash his teeth. Incidentally, he should not have been referred to as 'Taffy' since nicknames are forbidden in a monastery.

He worked through the postulancy and obtained the novice master's approval to enter his novitiate. He announced to all and sundry that he was going to take the name of the patron saint of Wales. This should have been kept secret as the bestowal of the name is the prerogative of the abbot, who usually consults the person concerned to see if he has a preference. Fortunately this statement by the future Brother David did not reach the ears of the abbot.

With his clothing as a novice, came his introduction to kitchen work, culminating in doing the job of cook for about seventy men, including the guests within the monastery. Our friend argued, of course, but the workmaster was unrelenting. He started at the bottom as second scullion, much to his disgust. To make matters worse, he had to stand on a box to wash up, as he had difficulty in reaching the deep stainless-steel washing-up tanks. The more mischievous souls took a delight in 'mislaying' his box.

On one occasion, Brother David chased his tormentors round the kitchen, brandishing a carving-knife. What he would have done if he had caught them is debatable, but they took no chances and kept the kitchen table between him and them just in case.

As a result of one such antic, Brother David lost his concentration. He had put a sack of potatoes in the potato peeler which was a carborundum-lined machine that revolved rapidly, rubbed off the peel and washed the waste out through a filter mesh, the water passing into the drain. Brother David had just started the machine when someone decided to pull his leg. This so annoyed him that he forgot the potato peeler and when he remembered to stop it, out came a batch of potatoes the size of small marbles.

Another incident happened when he was assistant cook. There was cod with potatoes and peas on the menu and the cook elected to fry the cod and chip the potatoes. The chipped potatoes had been prepared earlier by Brother

David and they were reposing in buckets of water, awaiting use. The cook had cut up the cod into the right number
of steaks to supply one per man and Brother David was
supervising the heating up of the cooking oil in two large
pans each about two feet by eighteen inches and over a foot
deep.

He had turned the gas a bit too high under one pan and
suddenly the oil reached its flash-point and burst into
flames. Brother David kept his head and immediately
banged on its airtight lid and turned out the gas under it,
which was the correct drill. The flames went out but,
without warning, the other pan decided to follow suit.
Brother David gave it the same treatment. He then opened
the lid of the first pan, preparatory to putting in the cod
steaks. He had the tray of cod steaks in his hands, when
the oil, which had not cooled below its flash-point temperature, suddenly burst into flames again spontaneously.
'Taffy' dropped the tray of cod steaks to attend to it and
when he collected the steaks which had rolled off the tray
he discovered he was one short. He found it behind the
cooker, covered in fluff and, as there were only just enough
to go round, he washed it under the tap and put it in the oil
to cook.

The next time that cooking oil was used, he annoyed the
cook by spitting into the pans to see if they were hot
enough to use. He explained that the best cooks always did
this and there was no danger of infection, since no 'bugs'
could live at that temperature anyway. He said the spit
evaporated with a hiss if the oil was hot enough. The first
cook said that even if this was done amongst the Dominicans, the Benedictines were not going to tolerate it.

There was a funny incident in the refectory one day. One
of the brethren had a peculiar habit of placing his knife
and fork on his plate when he had finished, with the tines
of the fork facing downwards. 'Taffy' watched this closely
and that evening in the common-room, he took the monk
aside and asked if he had been a freemason before he
entered the monastery. The reply being in the negative,
'Taffy' remarked that he had noticed this action with the
cutlery and thought that it was a masonic habit. This

caused quite a bit of hilarity. The joke was on the others though, since, when 'Taffy' finally left the monastery, it was understood that he became a freemason.

At one stage, the novice master heard of 'Taffy' being teased by the novitiate and he lectured them about it and rebuked them. But 'Taffy' himself invited it—he had let the initial remarks pass without taking any notice, the rest would have stopped teasing him. The same thing happened all the time, but others did not rise to the bait.

After novicing, Brother David managed to obtain the necessary chapter votes to enable him to enter into temporary vows, and, indeed, stayed long enough to reach his final year and join the senior common-room where he was well liked.

What went wrong we shall never know, but he showed signs of increasing uneasiness, and eventually asked for release before he had taken life vows.

It was better that it had happened at this stage, since the option to release him from temporary vows was in the hands of the abbot. Suffice it to say that our friend remained in his cell whilst the situation was being sorted out and then departed on the following day without any farewells. This was a pity, as the rest of the novitiate would have liked to have wished him God-speed.

Unfortunately, religious houses have a very nasty habit of making those who leave them feel like criminals in the condemned cell. They treat them like pariahs, which, to say the least, is an unChristian attitude.

BROTHER COLMAN

Sean Arthur O'Connel could not be anything but an Irishman with such a name so it is not surprising that he took the name of an Irish saint when he was noviced. He was somewhat unusual, as he was an Irish Anglo-Catholic and, as a general rule, the Irish are either fervent Roman Catholics or rabid Protestants. For this reason he was dubbed 'the mad Irishman' by the other postulants. His Irish brogue was not so evident as in many Irishmen since an educated accent came through.

When he became conscious of the 'call of the cloister' he

was in a quandary as the Irish Monasteries are Roman Catholic. I do not know of an Anglo-Catholic monastery in Ireland but, no doubt, having made this statement, I shall receive indignant letters from Anglo-Catholic monasteries all over Ireland. Such is life.

On presenting himself for admission, Sean, the son of an Irish schoolmaster, was nineteen years of age. He had received the equivalent of our grammar school education. The foundation was there and study would gain him entry as a choir monk. He had started as a clerk in a famous Irish bank on his seventeenth birthday but while his body was in the bank his mind was on becoming a monk. Having read Anson's *The Call of the Cloister* he had selected our monastery as his goal and had approached the abbot, initially by letter, which was passed on to the novice master. Arrangements were made for him to come over for a visit and talk with the abbot and novice master.

Returning after the usual two to three months 'cooling off' period he again pressed his plea to try his vocation, and his references from his church being satisfactory, permission was given for him to enter as a postulant.

He arrived at London Airport and was picked up in one of the monastery cars. Things happened when Sean was around that branded his memory indelibly on the mind for he had a knack for doing the wrong thing. He came on 5th January, the day before the Epiphany. There are several *dies non* and Long Recreation days attached to the period immediately after Christmas and it was evening before Sean had been settled in by the novice master. He was shown to his seat in the gallery of the chapel for compline and afterwards found his way into the corridor outside. He immediately approached a passing monk, and said in a voice that boomed in the deadly quiet of the Greater Silence, "What do I do now? I'm lost!"

Immediately scandalized eyes were turned upon him, and the monk to whom he had addressed his query put his finger to his lips and led him to the novice master.

The following morning, having been told to rise in time for prime, he went to his seat in the gallery and sat through the office. When he was collected by the novice master, Sean was himself scandalized to hear the murmur of conversation taking place in all parts of the monastery. He argued that if he could not speak last night, why was everyone talking this morning?

The novice master carefully explained the rule of silence and the Major Silence and explained that this being the feast of the Epiphany, it was a *dies non* and conversation would be allowed until the Major Silence after compline.

Sean went into the refectory for breakfast, and was gratified to find a large plate of cold ham waiting for him, with lashings of tea and coffee. There was plenty of bread and butter with marmalade to follow and his neighbour carried on a pleasant conversation with him. He retired feeling well filled and at peace with the world. If this was monasticism, he was all for it.

On leaving the refectory, he was claimed by a group of postulants and novices, who enquired if he would like to go for a walk after office and conventual Mass. They had permission to go out and the necessary senior had undertaken to accompany them. It only remained for Sean to get the permission of the novice master which was readily granted.

They set out along the river, where Sean was told they would swim in the summer. He thought to himself that this was all very pleasant and so different from the bread and water diet which he had envisaged in his own mind.

Arriving home in time for sext and none they found their places in chapel, and then in the refectory for lunch. There they were served with onion soup and bread, followed by roast beef and Yorkshire pudding and then there was a very passable treacle pudding, washed down with a very presentable hock, the whole accompanied by pleasant conversation. Again Sean congratulated himself upon having opted for the monastic life. Little did he know that there would be a dramatic change once the feast day was over.

In the afternoon there was a choice of another walk, this time within the extensive monastery grounds, a session of table tennis in the games room, or recordings of classical music in the music room. There were also, to his intense surprise, card games being played in the common-room.

Sean elected to play table tennis, at which he was a useful player. Afterwards he was ushered into vespers by the others, then into the refectory for tea. Here he found bread, butter, two kinds of jam, and an urn of tea. On a side trolley was a huge pile of slices of plum cake, with a notice which read 'One slice per man, please'.

After tea they amused themselves by playing chess, then there was the evening meal followed by compline and bed, where Sean slept the sleep of the just.

He was roused by the rising bell, but he ignored it on the novice master's instructions and got up in time for breakfast. This was a Long Recreation. His friends of the previous day were working at their allotted tasks in the morning, whilst Sean was given a session of instruction by the novice master. It appeared that Sean would not be expected to attend the night office at 5.00 a.m. for the first month of his stay in the monastery, but starting from the following Monday, he would have to arise at 5.00 a.m. when the rising bell sounded and do a session of housework—dusting and polishing corridors. He would also be allotted a Low Mass to serve at either 6.30, 7.00, 7.30, or 8.00 a.m. according to the Mass list posted on the notice-board. If it took place at 8.00 a.m. this would mean that he would miss prime and he would be expected to say it privately.

When in life vows a choir monk is bound to the office. Those offices which he misses in choir, he must say privately at his own convenience. Even monks who are ill say the whole office unless dispensed by the abbot on the advice of the infirmarian. The priests of the community say a Low Mass daily, and conventual Mass in rotation. Those monks who have not reached the priesthood serve at Mass daily and make their communion daily.

The novice master also informed Sean that he would be given a job by the workmaster during the work periods from the following Monday. Life was beginning to become a little more arduous.

Sean was instructed in how to process into his place in chapel and then sent into chapel for sext and none. In the refectory for lunch he found his seat and stood awaiting the entry of the abbot. Today there was a reader at the lectern and, after the abbot had said grace, the reader bowed and asked a blessing in Latin. He then read a passage of scripture and a section of the Rule of St Benedict, followed by the book which was currently being read in refectory, commencing from where he had stopped the last time. When the reader started on the book, since it was a Long Recreation following Epiphany, the abbot rang his handbell and the reader, having asked a blessing, again in Latin, left the lectern and took his seat for the meal. The community immediately commenced talking.

Today, the meal was simpler. Water took the place of wine and there were only two courses—minced beef with cabbage and mashed potatoes, followed by a good helping of apple tart and custard. Sean thought that they had quite a good cook anyway, the apple tart was delicious. He did not know that shortly, he would be the cook. After this 'talking' meal they were free to entertain themselves as yesterday.

In any event, Sean was weary and he retired to his cell for a rest on his bed. It was winter and cold outside but the central heating had been turned off at midday to conserve fuel. Sean found that lying on top of his bed, he needed his cloak to keep warm, even though he was fully dressed. He was to find out later that it can be very cold in the chapel at 5.30 a.m. Old hands always put on an extra sweater or two under their habit.

Time for evening meal came once again, with its accompaniment of bottled beer instead of the usual cocoa. After compline, there was once again the Greater Silence and then bed. Sunday passed in much the same manner. Many of the monks take the opportunity of having a bath on Sunday morning, if they are not on cooking or refectory duty. Everyone has a bathroom reserved for him one night per week, according to a rota posted on the notice-board. Nobody else uses that bathroom after compline. Monks are only allowed one bath per week unless on dirty work, they can take as many showers as they like—if they get to the shower-room first.

Monday morning dawned. Sean was sleeping peacefully when his door was flung open and a large handbell was rung violently in his ear—the rising bell. He nearly fell out of bed, but, managing to crawl out in the usual manner, he found an empty bathroom and after shaving and washing he joined the files of monks trooping along the corridor and downstairs in complete silence.

He located the corridor allotted to him and first swept the floor as instructed, then oiled it with a linseed-oil mop, and finally dusted the bookshelves with which the corridor was lined.

By this time, the monks were filing out of matins and lauds and he had to put his cleaning equipment away and hurry to the altar at which he was serving Mass. He lit the candles and assisted the priest to put on the vestments which were laid out in an alcove. He then preceded him to the altar.

After Mass he went straight to prime and then to breakfast, still wondering about the strange experience of saying Mass in the original Latin.

After breakfast, he was again claimed by the novice master, who took him to the workmaster to be given the work which he would perform after conventual Mass. He learnt that he was to join the painting squad, whose task, in a large country residence such as this was before becoming a monastery, was a job comparable with the Forth Bridge.

Next, he was taken by the novice master to the library where two books were selected for him, one a spiritual reading book and one for light reading. Everyone has to do spiritual reading in their cell between breakfast and conventual Mass; seniors select their own books but juniors have theirs selected for them. There is a separate light-reading section, where one finds books such as are found in a public library. There is usually also a section which is air-conditioned and shaded from sunlight. This contains many first editions and is a valuable part of the inheritance of the monastery.

After completing his spiritual reading for the day and attending conventual Mass, Sean changed into his brown boiler suit and reported to the painting squad. He was given a brush and a pot of paint, and started with five or six others to paint the corridor walls which seemed endless.

Sean worked in silence for some time, then remarked to his neighbour, "This is a turn up for the book! I never thought I would become a painter!" Before his neighbour could reply, the novice master's voice behind Sean said, "Mr O'Connel! A monk always keeps his mind trained upon God even when working. Unnecessary talking not only spoils your own recollection, but that of others also."

Sean said nothing, but he wondered how the 'old man' had managed to be in the wrong place at the wrong time. The novice master swept along the corridor and round the next corner.

Just before the angelus at noon, the painting party packed up and went to their cells to wash and change before sext and none, stopping to say the angelus when the big bell boomed out.

After sext and none, Sean was again collected by the novice master and taken into the *statio*, where the community was assembling to process into the refectory. Sean was shown his place and the procedure was explained to him. The monks formed two lines, facing inwards, and stood in silence awaiting the arrival of the abbot. The abbot led one line and the prior the other while the rest of the monks lined up in strict order of precedence.

When the abbot arrived, he took his place in the double line of monks, who all did a half turn and he led them into the refectory. Today, Sean was not so enchanted with the meal for the only drink was water and the meal consisted of two courses only, toad-in-the-hole with two vegetables and a portion of mince tart to follow. The menu and the portions were adequate but with a morning starting at 5.00 a.m. and a two-hour session of hard painting, after only a Continental-style breakfast, Sean was hungry. He realized too late that there was a platter of thick slices of bread with which to augment his meal.

After Sean had been in the community for four weeks, he was given a place in choir by the novice master and he had to lead the community into chapel, paired off with another postulant. This entry was carefully rehearsed with the novice master. The double line entered, proceeded as far as the double bank of choir stalls, genuflected to the altar, bowed to their partner and proceeded to their seats.

Sean entered with his partner and when they halted, he forgot all that he had been taught. He solemnly bowed to the altar, turned and genuflected to his partner and when his partner left to go to his seat, Sean was left standing, feeling foolish as he knew he had gone wrong somewhere. He bolted to his place, hoping that nobody had noticed. The novice master had though. Sean was patiently re-rehearsed and left to do the thing correctly next time.

By the time that Sean's postulancy came to an end, he was well versed in procedure, but he had the reputation of being the community clown, as he often did things wrong. Notwithstanding this however, it was obvious that he had a vocation and the novice master had no hesitation in recommending him for novicing.

He was accordingly measured for his first monastic habit by the monastery tailor and a day was appointed for the ceremony. He was allowed to write invitation cards for all his relatives and friends, and his guests sat in the guest narthex to witness his official entry into the community as a novice, when he abandoned his secular status and became a 'reverend' and a part of the community.

A week before the day, he went into retreat, conducted by the novice master and was due out of retreat immediately before the ceremony, so he was not available to greet his guests as they arrived, this being done for him by the novice master. The day before the ceremony, he had to change into his ordinary clothes, and he had to have the official tonsure.

The appointed time for the ceremony arrived. Vespers started in the usual way, while Sean, being debarred from entering the chapel, sat in the balcony overlooking the scene. Just as vespers was ending, Sean went down to the big doors where the community entered. These were closed against him. When the chant ceased, Sean banged on the doors which were opened by the novice master who led him

116

before the abbot, both genuflecting before the altar on the way.

Sean prostrated himself before the abbot, who said, "Arise, my son. What seek ye?" (I give a rough translation of the Latin, in which language the ceremony was conducted.)

Kneeling, Sean said, "I seek permission to try my vocation in this monastery, and to that end ask you to clothe me in the habit of a novice."

The abbot arose and conducted Sean and the novice master to the altar on which was placed the habit of a novice. The altar party then stripped Sean of his jacket and placed it folded beside the altar. This is a token stripping; in olden times the entrant was completely stripped of his secular clothing before being vested in monastic garb.

The abbot then said, "You see before you your own secular clothing and also the religious habit. I solemnly charge you to consider this. If you still wish to become a monk and to do battle with the devil in this monastery, you are now to choose which garments you desire. If you agree to try your vocation here, you must undertake to do battle according to the Rule of Saint Benedict and according to the rules laid down in the monastery. You are now to choose."

Sean stepped forward and, spurning his secular clothing, he selected the habit, which the abbot blessed and sprinkled with holy water. The altar party vested Sean in the monastic habit whilst the choir chanted the *Veni Creator Spiritus*. The abbot then gave Sean the kiss of peace, which he received in turn from the rest of the community, and he then announced, for the first time, the name by which the new novice would be known in religion, namely Brother Colman. Finally the novice master escorted Sean to his new seat in choir and the ceremony was concluded.

Afterwards, there was a reunion with family and friends, none of whom had seen him since his entry into the monastery more than six months before.

At tea-time, the refectory was thrown open to the

visitors and a substantial cold buffet tea was served. After walking in the grounds with his guests after tea, the novice showed his male guests over those parts of the monastery not normally on view to the public, and the female guests were shown over certain chapels which they would not normally see.

Workshops, workrooms and vegetable gardens were inspected, and all the visitors departed before the meditation period prior to the evening meal. After seeing his guests away, the novice retired to meditate, and the normal round of the monastery went on.

Brother Colman settled down to monastic life. After a month or two he was sent to a convent for his novice 'rest'—the first break that he had had after entering the monastery a year before. It should be noted that he was not allowed to go home for his rest until in temporary vows.

He was driven to the station in the monastery car and given a rail ticket and money for bus fares at the other end. It was his first experience of being in the outside world in a habit and he soon learnt that he was to be regarded as a being apart. His railway compartment was only occupied when the rest of the train was full and then the seat next to him was left vacant until there was no other available.

Seated on the platform at the London terminus awaiting his connection, he saw for the first time the then popular mini-skirt. A fellow passenger, noting his look, remarked, "Is not this a disgusting fashion, Father?" Turning, Brother Colman saw an elderly gentleman. He was rather tickled by the use of 'Father', to which, as yet, he was not entitled. He felt like telling the gentleman that he fully approved of the mini-skirt, but, lacking the courage of his convictions, he agreed with him. At that moment, the train arrived and he was saved from further remarks.

Brother Colman was accommodated in the priest's house, at the entrance to the convent and the nuns really spoiled him, giving him choice extra foods. He appreciated this as the cooking of the nuns was superior to that of the monks. He spent his week attending Mass and going for long walks in the surrounding countryside.

There was one charming concession of the Mother

Superior. Brother Colman asked her if it would be possible for him to lunch out one day as he had an aunt and uncle living within a short bus ride of the convent. Not only did she arrange this, but she invited the aunt and uncle to the convent for the day. They were given V.I.P. treatment and their meals were served to them in a private parlour put at Brother Colman's disposal. In addition, she arranged for a nun to take them on a guided tour of the convent, so that they saw many areas normally barred to visitors. They also saw the convent's silver and gold plate and many other treasures accumulated over the years—chalices, patens, and other altar plate along with vestments some of which had been made by the nuns and some presented to them.

Whilst Brother Colman was at the convent, the good nuns insisted on leaving him a selection of drinks in his room at the gatehouse. There was tea, coffee, cocoa, Horlicks, Ovaltine, Bovril, in fact everything that one could think of. There was also crockery, an electric kettle, a hotplate and a saucepan for the milk. Since milk was not delivered to the gatehouse Brother Colman was instructed to collect a large jug of it from the kitchen after compline. One day a gale-force wind rose up and he lost most of his milk, walking along the drive to the gatehouse in the dark.

Brother Colman was asked to be thurifer at Mass and he undertook this although he had not trained as a thurifer. The nuns did not know what they were letting themselves in for. The first full High Mass was enlivened by Brother Colman wandering off on his own with the thurible, after censing the priest at the wrong time and solemnly censing the community and visitors before returning the thurible to the priest. Everyone went along with this, bowing as he finished them, and he did not know he was wrong until the priest whispered to him as he returned the thurible.

As it happened, he was due for training as thurifer on his return to the monastery but this was not the first time that he had enlivened the proceedings. On one occasion, when he was acting as acolyte, he wandered off on his own, leaving his partner frantically signalling him to join up with him again.

On another occasion, during meditation, he fell asleep
in his stall and fell out of it with a crash, much to the
consternation of his neighbours, who thought he had suffered a heart attack.

Years later when he became the novice master of the
community the monks realized that anything might happen and postulants prepared themselves to carry him
round the chapel with them at their novicing ceremony,
instead of the other way round.

Once after ordination, he was acting as deacon at conventual Mass and he processed in with his stole round his
neck after the manner of a celebrating priest, rather than
over his shoulder as a deacon.

As the years went by, he gained a reputation for doing
the unexpected. On one occasion he was down to say Mass
at a local parish church (we sometimes acted as holiday
relief for outside clergy) and another of the brethren went
with him in the monastery car as driver and also to serve
for him at Mass. Owing to heavy traffic, they were late in
arriving and Dom Colman asked the other to light the
candles but leave him to find the lessons, in order to save
time.

They went to the altar. When the time came for one of
the lessons, Dom Colman turned to what he thought was
the second chapter of Isaiah which starts, "The word that
Isaiah the son of Amos saw concerning. . . ." Not having
time to read it through first, he started "I am the rose of
Sharon and the lily of the valleys. . . ." He had found chapter two of the previous book, the Song of Solomon. For
months afterwards he winced when anyone mentioned the
rose of Sharon.

On another occasion, Dom Colman was at a conference
and the whole of a small hotel had been booked for this. On
arrival, the receptionist asked if he would mind occupying
a double room with twin beds at the same charge, and
alone of course, as their single rooms had all been taken
up. He accepted this and had started to unpack, when a
colleague knocked on his door and said it was time they
went down for dinner. Dom Colman dropped everything
and left his clothing spread over both beds, including vest-

ments which he had brought to celebrate Mass.

On returning from dinner, he found that the chamber-maid had been in to turn down the beds, and had tidied up his things, turning down both the beds, and laying out his pyjamas on one bed and a lace-trimmed rochet on the other, evidently mistaking it for a lady's nightdress.

Dom Colman was incensed about the translation of plain-chant from its original Latin into English. He said he was tempted to do grievous bodily harm to the man who started to change and that it reminded him of a choir of nuns singing,

> Oh for a man
> Oh for a man
> Oh for a mansion in the sky!

He was a kindly man, and a great help to all the juniors who looked to him for guidance. Above all he was a deeply religious man, in spite of his absentmindedness. This was due to his strict recollection at all times. As far as I am aware, he is still livening up the proceedings in the monastery.

BROTHER WOLFSTAN

Denis Harold Pearson was the son of an Irish mother and an English father. His only Irish peculiarities were his Irish upper lip and his Gaelic temperament which occasionally came to the surface. He was entirely self-educated, since he had received little encouragement from his father regarding education.

His father had been a serving soldier in the First World War and he had been sent to Ireland during the rebellion. There he met his future wife and was married on demobilization. Like many men of that period, he found that his job had been filled in his absence. Two years of spasmodic unemployment followed, during which period Denis was born.

In the spring of 1921, the family fortunes were restored when the father secured a steady job. He had no qualifications except his Army training but settled with Morris Motors of Oxford, as a storeman. The car industry was expanding; Henry Ford produced his one hundred pound car and Morris capped it with a slightly better version for one hundred and ten pounds.

Denis shortly had a brother and a sister. The family were relatively prosperous but education was ignored. Denis was taken away from school at fourteen when already he had won a scholarship to the local grammar school. He was allowed to take this up only on the pleas of his headmaster. Later he won two university scholarships, one to Manchester and one to Oxford. The latter, his father refused to let him take up, as he said it was unfair to the younger brother, who was the dull one of the family. Again only the intervention of the school authorities, plus the pleas of his mother, persuaded the father to let him go to Manchester. Denis came down with a first-class Arts degree and a research scholarship enabling him to stay on for his Ph.D.

Despite pleadings, his father was adamant, that Denis must earn his living. Denis was lucky to get a job with Morris cars, despite his degree, since the depression was still biting. He resolved to save every penny that he could to fulfil his ambition to enter an Anglican theological college and his mother helped him, unbeknown to his father. After two or three years, Denis fulfilled his ambition and joined a college run by a monastic foundation, on an assisted grant.

Eventually he added ordination and a diploma in theology to his Arts degree. He was sent to a London parish as an assistant curate and there he met some of the monks from our abbey. He became an extern oblate and eventually applied for admission as a postulant.

Denis nearly came to grief in the early stages, for he was not prepared for the manual labour expected of all monks. He toiled on farm and in garden, workshop and kitchen. There were conferences with the novice master when he lost heart, but the latter was confident that Denis had a vocation.

He finally reached life vows and became Dom Wolfstan.

He was strictly a 'loner' which was probably due to the repression exercised by his father.

He was a great supporter of the move to prevent the liturgy being 'mangled' by the so-called 'reformers' and he retained the Latin Mass as long as he was able.

Being a lone wolf caused him to gain the undeserved reputation of expecting everything to be altered for his convenience. One incident will illustrate this. The individual cells, built in a monastery which was originally a stately home, are formed by partitioning off the large rooms. These hardboard partitions, packed with fibreglass, are not completely sound-proof. Dom Wolfstan being on the panel of priests who heard the confessions of the community, often used his cell instead of waiting for one of the much-used confessionals. Unless one spoke in a whisper, conversation could be overheard in the next cell and as is well known, the confessional should be strictly confidential. Dom Wolfstan wanted the monks each side to vacate their cells until he had finished. He appealed to the abbot who quite rightly refused to inconvenience two others to suit him and told him to wait for a vacant confessional.

Incidents like this did not endear him to his fellows, particularly as he kept to himself so much.

When the liturgy was changed from Latin to English, he refused at first to conform and used his own missal instead of the one provided. All the champions of the Latin Mass attended at his altar, leaving others denuded of communicants. When this reached the ears of the abbot, Dom Wolfstan was in hot water. It was put to him bluntly that the matter was one of obedience since the abbot upheld the changes. For a day or two Dom Wolfstan did not celebrate Mass. Then the abbot put him down to sing conventual Mass, in English of course, and he complied. The rest of the community observed with regret that they had been abandoned by their champion.

Considering his unbending self-sufficiency it was strange that he should be singled out for the unconscious humour of a child. It happened that as he stood waiting for a railway train one day, he came under the close scrutiny of a little girl, also awaiting the train with her mother. She walked round him, obviously puzzled by his habit and then engaged the reluctant monk in conversation of the, "Hello. What's your name. Where do you live?" type. He was a kindly man and would not deliberately snub a child, so he answered her questions. Then the girl produced the 'Sixty-four-dollar' question, "Do your knickers match your frock too?" Dom Wolfstan was taken aback, and the child's mother smiled apologetically and removed her offspring.

He repeated this joke against himself in the common-room, so it must have touched his sense of humour. He also told of another incident on a train. He was joined in a compartment by a young man who soon after said, "Excuse me, but we seem to be in the same line of business." Dom Wolfstan regarded him with interest, since he was in civilian clothes, and asked to what order he belonged. He replied that he was not a monk but was touring England with Billy Graham.

An interesting conversation ensued. They exchanged their religious viewpoints and the youngster said, of course, their religion was based on the Bible. Dom Wolfstan replied drily, that ours had a little to do with the Bible also. He produced his breviary and explained how it divided the psalms amongst the weekly offices, together with scriptural readings. He translated some passages for him and remarked upon two virtually identical psalms. The youngster hardly credited this until the monk told him to compare psalms fourteen and fifty-three. The young man said he had read the psalms many times but had never noticed the duplication.

The journey passed quickly and they both reached the conclusion that their brands of religion were closer than they had imagined. On parting, Dom Wolfstan invited the youngster to stay as his guest in the monastery. The youngster said that this might not be possible, much as he would have liked to, as they were due to return to the States.

Dom Wolfstan never took office in the monastery. Although he was a good monk, the abbot thought maybe, that he was too much of a solitary to direct others. He was also probably too much of a traditionalist. Traditionalists were not very popular with the abbot at the time, as he was bent upon fundamental changes in the liturgy.

Strangely enough, Dom Wolfstan confounded his critics by becoming extremely popular as a retreat conductor outside the monastery, where he had a free hand in deciding which form of service to use.

17

The Accountant and the Architect

BROTHER CYRIL

Kenneth Wilson Redding was an accountant, having followed his father into the family practice in Manchester. At twenty-two, he was already an oblate of the monastery and had considered the possibility of becoming a postulant. However, he had deferred this in accordance with his father's wishes as his father was not in robust health and Kenneth was needed in the practice. His only sister had died in infancy.

Kenneth lived in but not of his father's household, where he had his own suite of rooms. He could see no point in moving, as the house was in the city centre, near his office. One would not have realized that the house was there since it was down a private road between offices. Behind, a green park-like area contained the house, probably a relic of past years, before its neighbouring properties were demolished to build offices. The originally large staff of domestics was now reduced to a butler and a cook-housekeeper.

Kenneth always spent his annual retreat at the monastery while his parents went touring in Scotland, the staff went away on their annual holiday and the house was closed. The office was in the charge of their elderly chief clerk, who had been with them many years.

One year, while in mid-retreat, Kenneth was making his morning meditation in chapel when the guestmaster called him to an urgent telephone call from the chief clerk. Kenneth was surprised as the chief clerk had never had to call him before, usually things were neatly filed for attention on his return.

The chief clerk explained that it was not an office matter. He had received a message from the Cumberland Police that there had been an accident on the A6 near Carlisle, and Kenneth's parents were in a critical condition in Carlisle Hospital. Could Kenneth go there immediately?

As Kenneth returned to the guestmaster, the significance did not quite sink in. It could be his parents for his father always avoided motorways when touring.

The guestmaster could see that Kenneth was badly shaken. He arranged a meal for him and rang an hotel in Ilkley for him to stay overnight, dissuading him from driving through the night.

Kenneth was on the road by midday. After breaking his journey, he arrived at the hospital before noon the following day to find that his father had serious head injuries and was still unconscious. His mother, in another ward, was asking for Kenneth and her husband. The ward physician told Kenneth frankly that his father was gravely ill; the steering column had penetrated his chest, but it was the head injury that was critical. His mother should not be told. She had a back injury and although they had operated, they were afraid of paraplegia. She had not been told about this either. The accident had been caused by a motor-cyclist overtaking a car on a bend, so that his father, in swerving to avoid hitting him, had run into a tree instead.

After briefly visiting his mother, Kenneth was given permission to stay in the hospital. They were very kind, even finding him a quiet corner with a bed and supplying sandwiches and tea for which Kenneth was grateful.

During the night he lay back on the bed exhausted. He had just fallen into a fitful sleep when the nurse called him. He was with his father when he died without regaining consciousness.

His mother had slept well after Kenneth had seen her, much relieved in mind after his assurance that he had seen his father. Kenneth saw her for a few moments in the morning and she was comfortable and more cheerful, even talking of walking to the men's ward to see her husband "when her legs were a little stronger". She was told that on no account must she get out of bed, as movement could undo all the benefit of the operation.

The following day, since his mother was out of danger, Kenneth found a room at a nearby hotel, and that night had the best sleep in a week. He turned over the details of the funeral in his mind, and wondered when and how to tell his mother.

Washed, shaved, dressed and breakfasted, he was at the hospital by nine-thirty the following morning, only to find that there was no need to tell his mother about her condition. She was obviously much better, and had been experimenting, trying to move her toes. She was an intelligent woman and she had challenged the ward sister with the conclusion she had reached. The ward sister admitted that they were afraid of paraplegia, but could not say definitely until things healed.

Kenneth thought to himself that part of his problem had solved itself, but he still could not decide when to tell her about his father. The problem was eased by the specialist deciding to move his mother to a hospital in Manchester which specialized in paraplegic cases.

His father's funeral had been held up by the coroner but he could now attend it without his mother asking questions since she had been moved by the time that clearance came. Kenneth had his father's body taken to Manchester for burial, as he knew that his mother would wish to visit the grave and this would make it easier for her.

He felt very depressed as he attended the funeral. The office was closed and the staff, together with the domestics, were present at the service. Friends had not been informed because of the danger of their contacting his mother, and the family had no relatives in England.

The difficulty was keeping friends from his mother. She was content when told that her husband was not yet fit to move, but hurt because her friends did not come to see her.

The specialists decided that nothing further could be done for her. It would be necessary to have a wheelchair and lifting apparatus to give her a measure of independence. When she demanded to be taken to her husband,

Kenneth had to tell her the truth. She received the news stoically and asked Kenneth to leave her alone for a while. When she rang her bell after about ten minutes, she was in control of herself again, and calmly and sensibly made plans for the future.

Kenneth was now head of the firm and he could see that there was no chance of his entering the monastery immediately, but in the event, he was able to enter five years later, when his mother died prematurely, probably as a result of her condition. He had done his duty and seen her through to the end.

He presented himself at the monastery just after his thirtieth birthday and passed through postulancy, novitiate and temporary vows in an exemplary manner. He obviously had a vocation and was life professed just after his thirty-seventh birthday and ordained two years later.

After ordination, he interested himself in the reunion of Christendom and in connection with this he was often sent to Continental monasteries for conferences. On one of these visits, he was leaving from London Airport. The monastery car taking him to London had been badly delayed by traffic, and he arrived late. He rushed his baggage through on arrival, as the other passengers were boarding the plane, and he was being urgently 'paged' over the tannoy.

As he hurried out to the plane, a young woman obviously mistaking him for a Roman priest, fell on her knees before him and said in an Irish accent, "Bless me Father, for I have sinned." Being in too great a hurry to explain, he made the sign of the cross over her and muttered a Latin blessing. He explained that his plane was leaving, and she was satisfied. It was not until he was seated on the plane that he realized that he had given her the blessing for a new building.

Dom Cyril as he now was, led an exemplary monastic life. He had written a book on theology, and was preparing another when an unfortunate incident occurred.

It is customary for a monastery to gather round it a group of oblates, mostly men, who can participate fully in the monastic life. There are some women oblates, who feel that they can derive greater benefit from being associated with a community of monks where the priests are integrated. When making their retreats, they live in a nearby convent, spending the daytime in the monastery for instruction. They are directed by one of the monks.

One such woman oblate was directed by Dom Cyril. The lady had a 'bachelor' flat in Kingston and she sometimes invited Dom Cyril for a meal as he passed through on business. This was unwise, but Dom Cyril saw nothing wrong. However, tongues started to wag as they will where the Church is involved.

One day, Dom Cyril received a rather hysterical telephone call from the lady, asking him to call as soon as possible. There had been a break-in at her flat and although not much had been stolen, it had considerably unnerved her. As she had no relatives to call upon, she had rung Dom Cyril. He left immediately and arrived about tea-time, the arrival being noted by the curtain-twitching neighbours. These good folk kept watch and were scandalized when the car was there until late at night and still more so when it was still there the following morning.

Dom Cyril had rung the abbot to tell him that there was an emergency and it was necessary for him to stay at the home of an oblate, not mentioning that it was a female oblate. This point militated against him at the subsequent enquiry.

On his return to the monastery, Dom Cyril reported to the abbot, omitting to say that there had been only the two of them in the flat, but explaining that the lady was in a hysterical condition and had begged him to stay. He had spent a very uncomfortable night in an armchair.

Here the matter rested until the abbot received a particularly nasty anonymous letter. He usually ignored unsigned letters, but this time he asked for Dom Cyril's comments. Dom Cyril told the whole story, omitting nothing. He still maintained that the lady could not be left and that he had slept in the armchair; he had left as soon as it was daylight. Knowing Dom Cyril, I am quite prepared to believe him, as was the abbot.

However, the abbot was extremely annoyed that Dom Cyril should have been so foolish. Dom Cyril admitted this, but denied anything improper. The abbot called a few seniors for advice and it was agreed to ignore the letter. They accepted Dom Cyril's explanation but censured him for foolishness. They decided to send him away for a year to the daughter house in Kenya, where they ran a missionary school. He returned a year later considerably chastened. The abbot interviewed the lady and suggested that she transfer to a convent for religious instruction.

As far as is known, Dom Cyril continues to live an exemplary monastic life, no doubt remembering the unfortunate incident when called upon to direct a lady oblate.

It seems the public are always ready to criticize the Church and invent extraordinary stories of the 'goings on' in monasteries. I admit there is the occasional failure or scandal, which receives the maximum publicity in the media. The incidence of these is, however, much lower than outside the Church, which is only as it should be.

BROTHER LUKE

Samuel Keith Wroughton presented himself as a postulant at the age of twenty-six, just prior to the outbreak of war in 1939. One of his critics said that he had joined to evade military service, but I know that this was not so. He had received a good, minor public school education and he was a qualified architect when he entered.

Samuel had been brought up as an Anglo-Catholic. During his early years, he had never had a regular girlfriend, since he spent all his time studying. His thoughts were diverted from marriage later, when he considered becoming a monk.

He was generally a placid man but he exploded when he was aroused. I well remember how incensed he was when we were discussing the breakdown of the liturgy by so-called 'reformers'. One of the younger brethren was the ringleader and I remarked that if he carried on he could become the future abbot. Dom Luke's reply was, "If he does, he will find himself sitting on the abbot's bloody

131

throne on his tod! He is going the right way to lose the community as well as the liturgy!" Not a very monk-like pronouncement—I trust that it was confessed later.

People are shocked if monks use bad language, but remember that monks are ordinary human beings, who are there to reform their lives.

Dom Luke went straight through to life profession without faltering. He has books upon the liturgy to his credit probably this is why he finds disruption so distasteful. He commented that, as I too have found, the use of universal Latin is advantageous. When abroad, even if not conversant with the language, I could always follow the Latin Mass. Dom Luke said that the new communities revised their Rule at the wish of their founder. Not much hope for us then, unless we resurrect St Benedict.

He had a sense of humour and said the monastery laundry was determined that he should have no buttons on his undervest. Each time buttons vanished, he sewed on new ones but these were either broken or burnt off by the ironer. He tried linen-covered metal buttons but these were pulled out by the roots, each with a bit of undershirt attached. He gave it up and changed to singlets in the summer. But when winter came again, he viewed his buttonless undershirts with distaste. Then the idea dawned! He stitched them up and dragged them over his head. Game and set to him! He said the roller iron was making grumbling noises thinking up ideas of defeating him.

He complained of the 'emancipation' of the novitiate. There was a time when a novice was not allowed in the library, now he could not get near the books for them. Lay brothers were vanishing, now they all wanted to be choir monks—probably we are abandoning Latin and Greek for this. Why not simply admit them to chapter? It is invidious that they have no say in monastic government. Silence used to be unwavering, but now even the Trappists chatter.

Fraternization with guests? More friendly probably, but do guests in retreat then have to wear a label round their necks?

Provision of coffee after Mass? Helpful if guests have driven far without breakfast, but some monks make a meal of it.

The rule of the Abbot? At one time the abbot was a total despot, with the power of life and death. Imagine how long he would last if he ordered a flogging today, not to mention an execution.

The Rome Council of abbots? They ordered the transition to English. Publishers stopped publishing office books. Thus we have to produce our own typed versions and almost need a wheelbarrow to carry our folders about. Fortunately we are still permitted to use our Latin pocket breviary for private recitation.

So he carried on about the unwelcome changes. He worked outside amongst our dockland 'dropouts' and went fearlessly alone where police patrolled in pairs. He went in the car alone to rescue the dropouts and brought them back to be 'dried out', until one turned nasty in the car. We were then ordered to go out in pairs in the car.

One of his rescues nearly came to grief. He brought into the guest-house two drug addicts who claimed they had been through medical withdrawal. But later, we found out that they had somehow organized a supply of drugs in the guest-house. Dom Luke was furious. He bundled them into the car and dumped them where he had found them. We could have been prosecuted for having drugs on our premises.

Considering his compassion for this kind of victim, he would have been freer in an open order, but he seemed content if the abbot allowed him to do this kind of work. He had a flair for finding good works and even tried his hand once, quite successfully, at marriage guidance.

His love for the traditional liturgy brought him to grief. After many stormy sessions in chapter he opted for the traditionalists. No one knows what caused him to make the final decision, but he applied for temporary exclaustration and when this was granted he went to work in a dockland parish.

After six months, he applied for dispensation from his monastic vows which would free him for the secular priesthood, without any connections with the monastery. This went through and two years after this I heard that he was married and had settled down as a priest in a London parish.

I would imagine that Dom Luke would find quite a successful niche for himself as a parish priest, with his flair for good works and his quiet sense of humour, which no doubt would come out in his sermons.

Once in the common-room, he gave us an example of this. The question of sudden spectacular conversions to the faith was under discussion. Dom Luke said his was a case in point. All ears pricked up. He said that before he became a Christian, someone deliberately splashed water over his head. He was just going to strike out in anger, when he suddenly remembered that he was only eight weeks old. He departed rapidly as the penny dropped.

18

Disruption and Tranquillity

BROTHER BENEDICT

Paul Grant Shutler, the nephew of a bishop, came from a wealthy family and was educated at Eton and Cambridge. Called up for National Service after the war, he entered as a private and left as a private which should have flashed the warning light when he came to the monastery.

After military service, he went to a theological college and obtained a degree in theology, entering the abbey immediately after graduation.

He was very unobtrusive during his novitiate and temporary vows. He was good on the manual labour side, having the constitution of the Rugby player that he was. He was a six feet two and Nordic in appearance and although he had stamina, he made shocking bloomers in other fields.

We had received some lead sheeting for capping unused chimneys after the removal of the pots. Dom Benedict went on the flat roof with others to do the job but unfortunately, he omitted to secure one sheet. During the gale, this blew off and landed crumpled in a corner, where it lay undiscovered. A lay brother was on the roof two weeks later and found the lead. Inwardly branding Dom Benedict as a 'silly twit' for allowing the spare sheet to blow about until it was useless, he removed it and put it in the scrap-lead bin.

During the next heavy rain, the chimney leaked and the absence of the sheet was noticed and enquiries instituted. The lay brother explained and Dom Benedict blamed him for including it in scrap which had now been sold. This was irrelevant since the sheet was useless when picked up.

Another sheet of lead was procured, and a chastened Dom Benedict replaced it. Apart from this incident, Dom Benedict's work did not again come under criticism. He made sure of that by always letting someone else take the responsibility.

After life profession, he really made headway and used his influence to push his ideas through. His first clash was with the novice master over reciprocal visits with the novices of other monasteries which he had arranged. The novice master, rightly, thought that novices should not leave their monasteries until grounded in monastic protocol. In fact, going outside is disturbing for the new novice. However, these visits continued with the abbot's blessing and, every month, the novitiate was either taken to another monastery or their novices brought to us.

The next clash was with one of the most senior of the monks. Dom Benedict suggested in chapter that the office in Latin was a "load of old rubbish" and that it should be in the vernacular. The venerable monk was appalled. He had joined the community at eighteen and he was now nearly ninety, and during all that time, he had said the Latin office. Why change now? There was an argument and it appeared that most wanted to retain the Latin.

The abbot announced that he was in favour of the change and that the matter would be put to the vote but anyone voting against the change would incur his "grave displeasure". He pointed out that he could order the change instead of taking a vote on it. This was true and at the show of hands not many had the courage to vote against it.

The community lost its Latin, much to the consternation of many. The weekly choir practice became twice weekly, then daily . But the chant continued to grind to a halt. The novitiate were drilled after each office in preparation for the next one and then the abbot ordered the attendance of seniors as well. The routine of the monastery was being disrupted to keep the office going, with its seven choir practices weekly.

Dom Benedict's laxity bred laxity in the novitiate. For example, it happened that he had to pass the '*Pax*' or Kiss of Peace on to a novice. To the uninitiated, this means that the senior puts his hands on the shoulders of the junior, saying, "Peace be with you", to which the junior should reply, "And with thy spirit" at the same time placing his hands upon the elbows of the senior. On this occasion, Dom Benedict said, "Peace be with you" and the junior replied, "And with you Guv." As a novice, I would have been disciplined but Dom Benedict repeated it as a joke. There were rumblings of rebellion, quelled by the abbot on the grounds of obedience.

Dom Benedict, who had passed his ordination examination prior to entry, was now ordained, and he immediately pointed his guns at the Mass. The campaign was introduced a little at a time. The first step was the conversion of everything into English which took over a year, but was forced through by the abbot. The next attack was on the ceremonial vestments which were laid aside on a 'year's trial' but all knew that we had lost them for ever.

The attack rested for a full year, then it was announced that the Mass would be abandoned in favour of the new Series Two edition of the Mass. The chant broke down completely. The distortion was churned out without sense of timing or music. Unfortunately, those who hated the changes could not stay away, as in a parish, and this led many monks to request exclaustration and secularization. It was pointed out that the Roman Church was also in the throes of change.

The general exodus started. First novices and monks in temporary vows left, followed by the young ones in life vows. These were young men who could make a fresh start in another field but the old ones had little choice. As one of them pointed out, "What have I got? I have only my ordination to fall back upon after nearly fifty years in the monastery." He went on to say that even if he got a job as a curate, he could not live on curate's pay at that time, unless he had a private income. He was not likely to find a living quickly at his age.

By and large, our Dom Benedict had the doubtful distinction of removing more monks from the monastery than any other cause in its long history. As his influence increased, he caused other innovations such as inviting a 'pop' group to enliven the Mass, and introducing Negro Spirituals, and to crown it all, finished with a party of students, some of them girls, 'doing a turn' in the chapel within the sanctuary. There is an old-established tradition in the Catholic Church that females are not permitted in the sanctuary which is one of the arguments against the ordination of women in the church.

This episode led to a protest to the bishop by one of the guests. There was no apparent reaction, but, significantly, it did not happen again. The diocesan bishops seem to be a little nonplussed in dealing with a monastery; Anglican monasteries seem to be a law unto themselves.

The crisis resolved itself unexpectedly. The sub-prior of the daughter-house in Kenya was suddenly taken ill with an obscure tropical disease and he died on his way back to England. The vacancy was filled by the abbot sending out Dom Benedict.

Most of the community regarded it as divine intervention. Much more of his interference would have split the community wide open. The tragedy was that the community was left depleted in numbers and with a hopelessly mutilated liturgy, which it would be impossible to repair with any degree of success, unless it were scrapped and a fresh start made. A visitor to the monastery told me later that their liturgy was still in a state of flux.

BROTHER FABIAN

Philip James Harris was already ordained when he entered the community. He was the son of a parish priest and had a brother, also ordained, who taught in a theological college.

In some communities he would not be called Brother, in view of his ordination, but would be called Father. In this community he was normally called Brother, but was Father when exercising his priestly duties. As a postulant he was Father Harris then Brother Fabian as a novice. After life profession, he operated as a full community priest but before that could only celebrate Low Masses.

Priest entrants do not settle to monastic life as easily as laymen, probably because they are used to a privileged position as a priest in the world outside.

Philip served his postulancy and novitiate without incident and was accepted for temporary profession. I shall describe here the form the ceremony takes.

The candidate goes into retreat a week before the ceremony, under the master of juniors. At the ceremony, he takes his place in choir for conventual Mass, which is sung by the abbot. At the offertory, after the abbot has sung the offertory sentence but before the choir has sung the response, the master of juniors brings forward the candidate who prostrates himself before the abbot. The abbot bids him rise, and reminds him that he stands in the presence of God and asks if he is prepared to promise stability, obedience, and the monastic way of life, and reminds him that he will be mocking God if he acts contrary to his vows. The candidate reads his petition aloud to the assembly. He vows obedience to the abbot and his successors, stability, and conversion of life, the latter embracing poverty and chastity.

The petition is signed on the altar by the monk, and countersigned on the gospel book by the abbot. The chapter clerk and the master of juniors also sign.

The monk then sings his *Suscipe,* so called from the initial word of the Latin text. This is sung three times on a progressively higher note, each time nearer the altar. The English rendering is, "Uphold me O Lord according to Thy word, that I may live. Let me not be confounded of my hope."

In temporary profession, the novice's scapular and belt are removed and replaced by the ankle-length scapular and leather strap of the professed monk. The abbot bestows the choir cowl.

At solemn life profession, the monk wearing these already, proceeds to the next stage of 'Bidding the Bedes'. He kneels before the different sections of the choir in turn, asking their prayers. The abbot then bestows the kiss of peace, which is given by the rest of the community in turn. The newly professed then places a host on the paten, which he will receive at Communion. After this he is led to his stall in choir.

At life profession, the candidate lies under the funeral pall and the funeral candles are placed around him, while the choir chants the litanies for the dead, until the pall is whipped off, usually by the newest entrant, and the choir chants, "Arise and Christ shall shine on you". This is symbolic of death to the old life and resurrection into the new.

Before life profession, the monk must be interviewed by the bishop of the diocese and the bishop visitor of the monastery.

When Dom Fabian reached life profession, he specialized in oblate retreats and he often helped the oblate master to organize the complex oblate day. He spent time lecturing in the various dioceses and was responsible for introducing many new vocations. He watched postulants come and go with interest. One arrived whom he had seen appear as an aspirant when he had stayed a few days in the guest-house. It is strange how different the monastic life seems viewed as an aspirant and as a postulant. On entry, illusions and delusions are shattered and the life seems less romantic. Nobody from the outside can have the faintest idea what the life is like.

Dom Fabian wondered if this one would make the grade to life profession, a minimum of four and a half years hard grind.

New postulants are allowed a few days to get the feel of the place. One once remarked that he wished he had something to do. Dom Fabian replied that this would come soon enough. The next day Dom Fabian saw him on hands and knees scrubbing out a lavatory, and asked him if he was satisfied now. The reply was a cryptic, "It will do!"

When Dom Fabian was new, he once answered the outer doorbell and there stood his mother. He was so surprised that he was speechless. She said, "I was passing in the car unexpectedly, and wondered if I might have a word with my son." She had not recognized him in his cassock and he had just had his hair cut by the monastery 'barber'. Realizing that there was no catastrophe involved, the son re-

140

gained his composure and said, "I think that can be arranged Madam, as you are speaking to him!"

Dom Fabian's former bishop was very absent-minded. He generally used a bicycle for short distance visits but on one occasion he had walked instead. On leaving, seeing a bicycle outside, he mounted it and rode away. His secretary received a telephone call to say that the bishop had 'borrowed' the cycle and the owner had not been quick enough to stop him. "Dear me," said the bishop, "I must return it personally and apologize." When he returned the bicycle, the owner offered him a sherry. On leaving, he had mounted the bicycle again and was pedalling away until restrained by the shouts of the owner.

Another of his interests was exorcism. In this field he was walking a tightrope, since the practice is rather frowned upon in some sections of the Anglican Church. As he said, even if one keeps an open mind the friendly or malicious atmosphere can be detected, which is dispelled by exorcism. Exorcism is regarded as legitimate by the Church today.

Having done his stint of cooking and manual labour, he took over the kitchen supplies and, by buying in bulk, effected immense savings. He also resurrected the manufacture of incense and built up a thriving business with Catholic parishes throughout the country. He started making synthetic icons. Genuine icons are worth a lot of money, being hand-painted on wood by orthodox monks who go into a long retreat before painting, to purify themselves before depicting the life of Christ. These icons are hung on their icon screen and are revered like our crucifixes. It is possible to buy transfers, which, mounted on wood, make a passable reproduction. I have in fact seen one of these for sale in an antique shop as the genuine article but it was removed on my intervention.

These secular pursuits are sometimes criticized as being too worldly for monasteries but I cannot accept this, for St Benedict laid down that monks should live by the labour of their hands. Dom Fabian makes an excellent contribution to the income of the monastery.

Apart from his activities mentioned above, Dom Fabian

was interested in the rescue of 'drop-outs' from the London dockland. Although not a car driver, when instructions were given to go out in the cars in pairs, he volunteered to go out with a driver and he spent a lot of his time working amongst the drunks and drug addicts. He was responsible for the rehabilitation of many of them, seeing them established again as useful members of society.

19

The Orate Fratres

Having remarked on the secular pursuits, it is appropriate to mention the spiritual pursuits of the monk.

Accepting that the main function of the monastery is to pray for a world which has forgotten how, the monk must be informed of events outside the monastery if he is to pray for them. This information is obtained in several ways. Firstly, from the letters written to the community. Secondly, from monitoring radio and newspaper reports by an appointed monk who listens to news bulletins and extracts items from newspapers. Thirdly, telephone calls are received and acted upon. The above are all collected and posted on typed cards on a board called *Orate Fratres* or "Pray Brethren" and the cards are reviewed daily. The monks consult this board before meditation, private prayers or Mass.

The routine of private prayer in the revised liturgy is organized under about five headings. This, as I and many others see it, is the one and only good point of the so-called 'reformed' liturgy.

The *Orate Fratres* board has columns, one for the souls of the departed and one for those who have lost their faith. Apart from these columns, each day has its specific 'prayer thought': Sundays are for the people, (*pro populo*); Mondays for the clergy; Tuesdays for our confraternity of monks, oblates, associates and benefactors; Wednesdays for the propagation of the Faith; Thursdays for the re-union of Christendom; Fridays for our Queen and country and Saturdays for the increase of vocations to the religious life.

The Thursday intercession is strengthened by the burning of the "Thursday candle" before the statue of Our Lady in the Lady Chapel. This is especially for the reunion with Rome. In the same way our one hour "Exposition of the Blessed Sacrament" on Thursdays—the Holy Hour—is dedicated especially to the reunion of the Churches. There is also a monthly list of obituaries posted, and Low Masses are said for these.

The requests for prayers are many and varied, ranging from heart-rending cases to the trivial (in my opinion) requests for people to pass examinations or obtain appointments. I always feel that one should not ask God for things which involve personal fitness. If worthy, one will pass the exam or obtain the appointment if not, one is not suitable anyway.

A heart-rending case which springs to mind was that of a child of two suffering from incurable cancer. Then there are the matrimonial cases and the children involved. Having had a blissfully happy home life and two wonderful if strict parents, one cannot really feel the plight of these children, who must feel lost and unwanted. People write asking for prayers for bereavement or financial difficulties. We also pray for suffering humanity resulting from disaster, famine or war. Finally, we pray for the increasing numbers that fall away from religion.

One of the convents has a different approach to prayer for others, common amongst the Trappists—the perpetual watch before the altar where the sacrament is reserved. In this convent, day and night, there is a nun at prayer at the desk where a book of intercessions is kept. The watch is only broken when the community are chanting office and are, therefore, all at prayer anyway.

We are often told that the 'open' orders, which spend all their time in external work, are the only worthwhile ones. People can see the sense of a community like the Edgware Nuns, who care for the disabled, or the Cenacle Sisters of the Roman Communion, whose life work is running a retreat and conference centre. The latter are often jokingly called the "Cynical Sisters" which they accept philosophically.

As a boy, I was taught that "Satan trembles when he

sees the weakest sinner on his knees". Ask any of the people for whom prayers are offered. Many will tell you that they are miraculously delivered from their extremity. Coincidence? These cases are too numerous to be accounted for by coincidence or the law of averages.

Some will point out that many people have died when prayers were offered for their recovery. True, but who can expect that prayer and the will of God will coincide in every case? Prayer contrary to the will of God can never succeed. Our Lord taught us to pray "Thy will be done". and himself prayed that he would not have to undergo crucifixion, but, "Nevertheless, not my will, but thy will be done". His prayer was not answered as he would have wished it. If it had been, mankind would still remain unredeemed.

Unfortunately, there seems to exist a shyness or reticence to discuss the activity of prayer. Prayer should be a natural and routine process, like visiting the doctor for advice in sickness, or for preventative medicine.

A rather unfortunate slip-up happened in one monastery of my acquaintance. The names of three oblates had been sent in for prayers, as they were all in hospital, one for an operation, one because of a motor accident and one because of illness. Their cards should have been placed in the "Prayers for the sick" section, instead, they were inadvertently placed in the R.I.P. column. For several days, until the mistake was discovered, the monks were busily praying for the repose of their souls, when they should have been praying for their recovery. The monks who knew them were rather shocked as it was known that the motor-accident victim had only been kept in hospital for observation after a fracture of the femur. As it happened, this was rather amusing, but it could have caused distress to relatives, had they known.

I can hear my agnostic reader commenting that monks are wasting their time in prayer. Do you think so? I can recall a self-professed atheist commenting during a discussion on the subject, "If that is how things stand, then thank God I am an atheist!"

20

Two Noteworthy Monks

BROTHER ATHANASIUS

Frederick Leslie Allan was born in Rhodesia of second-generation Rhodesian farming stock. From the beginning he made it clear that he supported Ian Smith in keeping the blacks out of power in Rhodesia, on humanitarian, practical and Christian grounds. He said we were misinformed and that the bulk of the blacks were not intelligent enough to vote. There had been vicious and unprovoked attacks on white farms, involving murder. He deplored the fact that anyone not having first-hand experience of the conditions should presume to pass judgement.

We were discussing this once in the junior common-room but were stopped by the novice master on the grounds that it was a political issue. This was unfortunate as we were being given first-hand information. I can only add that I have since heard the same opinions expressed several times, when in South Africa. Also I could see that blacks were better off segregated and able to enjoy their own culture.

Frederick had been educated at a good public school in England, as had his brother. The boys did not go on to university but went instead to an agricultural college to study English methods.

Frederick had developed an interest in the Catholic Church whilst at school and had stayed in the monastery guest-house during his holidays. While at the agricultural college he decided to apply for admission to the monastery. He had an aunt living in England, a lady of independent means, with whom he stayed. When she heard of his entering the monastery, she is on record as saying, "Poor boy!

Poor boy! Fancy, after entering those dreadful doors, never to see a woman's face again." How wrong she was—he later spent several rests with her.

His father reluctantly gave in and Frederick entered into his postulancy with enthusiasm. He was a robust boy, and he readily accepted the alternation of study and manual labour. His education stood him in good stead and he digested the Latin and Greek, monastic protocol and monastic history.

He took the name of Athanasius when he was noviced. He was popular as he was an extrovert and a championship-class chess player. The latter led to a humorous incident at the chapter of faults. He had dropped a chess piece, a knight, and broken it so he stood up and announced in chapter, "I have knocked the head off a knight's horse." There was a guffaw, quelled by a glance from the novice master, who, when the chapter was over, enquired what he meant.

On his acceptance for temporary vows his brother sent him a large collection of slides of the Rhodesian farm and surrounding country and he was given permission to show these on the projector during recreation. They were extremely interesting.

In his last year, he was appointed as a driver since he was expert with car, lorry or tractor because of his farming background. On call, he had to watch the Journey Board to see what journeys were required and he had also to do the circular tour of the surrounding convents, dropping and picking up priests who were saying Mass there. Besides these duties, he always met certain trains at the local railway station, taking and fetching community and visitors.

On one of his driving duties, a curious thing happened. He had taken the van with another monk, to collect the weekly groceries, and they loaded these and some fruit and vegetables including several hands of bananas. There was no partition between the seats and the goods space and, on the return journey to the monastery, the passenger happened to glance down and then said in a quiet but imperative voice, "Pull in. Stop. Get out quickly and shut your door!" When the van stopped, the passenger did the same. Brother Athanasius wanted to know what the urgency was so the passenger explained that he had spotted a huge red hairy spider. They decided to kill it in case it was poisonous and having procured a spanner from the tool-box in the side of the van, they opened a door gingerly. They soon spotted it and although it moved with alarming speed, they managed to kill it at last. It was huge, fully four inches across, and covered in red hair.

On their return, they rang the village store in case there were any more. The proprietor explained that it must have come with the bananas as they had found them before. The monks were wise to kill it as it could have been poisonous.

Every year the novice master took a party from the junior common-room for an outing to visit places like cathedrals, Stonehenge or the Cotswolds for a day tour, starting after conventual Mass. Packed lunches were taken and flasks of coffee and tea. The monastic office was said at suitable stopping places. The senior members were taken by Brother Athanasius.

They were usually invited to tea by a convent *en route*. On one occasion Brother Athanasius's party was returning late as the nuns had served tea late. By about 9.00 p.m. it was getting dark, and they still had fifty miles to go.

On these occasions, the senior monk carries a purse of money in case of need, and the monks tried to persuade him to stop for half a pint and some cheese sandwiches at a village pub as they had missed the evening meal. There was a shout of "Here's one!" and the driver pulled up in the car park. It was rather an incongruous sight to see six monks vanish into the pub. However, a private room was asked for and soon beer and cheese sandwiches were forthcoming.

One of the monks was teetotal, and had lemonade, and it was decided that he should report their return to the abbot, whilst the others stood back. All went well and the abbot did not apparently smell their breath. However, the following morning the abbot passed Brother Athanasius in the corridor and asked how the outing had gone, saying with a twinkle in his eye, "How did the beer and cheese supper go down?" We have often wondered how he found out.

Convents often rely upon monasteries to provide priests and altar party for their festivals or profession ceremonies. Dom Athanasius as he then was, often drove such parties.

Dom Athanasius was very fond of children, and he organized a visit to us of the children from the children's home run by a convent. Luckily it was a hot sunny day and the children enjoyed games and sports he had organized on the lawn and finished with a picnic tea in the shade of a huge oak on the lawn. Dom Athanasius worked hard to provide party items dear to the hearts of children.

Less than an hour after we had waved them off in their coach, we had cleared the lawn and were washing up in the kitchen when we were startled by a tremendous noise. We all ran out thinking a plane had crashed but instead we found that a huge branch had fallen off the oak tree just where the children had been eating. It had partly buried itself in the lawn and must have weighed several tons. It was providential that the children had gone. In the interests of safety, we decided that the tree must go. It was weeks before the big hole was filled in and turfed.

It was customary for a monk to be ordained after life vows then, but individuals could decline. Thus Dom Athanasius was never ordained.

The Anglican Church recognizes only three strata of ministry, deacons, priests and bishops. The Romans have seven or more e.g. doorkeepers, acolytes, subdeacons, deacons, priests and bishops. Anglican monks pass the lower orders automatically, formal ordination starting with Deacon, although from the novitiate they are entitled to be addressed as "Reverend".

Five years after life profession, Dom Athanasius was allowed to visit Rhodesia—most monks from abroad are allowed to visit their homes.

One of Dom Athanasius's pet aversions was to hear many of the youngsters in the community holding forth after the manner of youth today, using words without fully understanding their origin or meaning. Words such as charismatic, eschatological, antinomy and tautology. Dom Athanasius discoursed upon their Greek or Latin origin and said it annoyed him intensely to hear youngsters using words either incorrectly or with an obvious misunderstanding of origin.

Not that he was anti-youth in any way. He said that some people maintained that youngsters today were lacking in both moral fibre and mental stability but he strongly opposed this view. Likewise, he opposed the idea that young people are perfect. Whilst pleased to see that they are more self-confident than we were at their age, he deplored their view that all good ideas stem from them.

He said that when we were young we had had to refrain from expressing our opinions as we were considered to be lacking in experience. Now we had reached maturity the younger generation thought we were too senile and that experience counted for nothing.

I believe that the trouble is that today's youth have never been tested. In our day, the country was just recovering from one war when we were forced to fight another. People said of us that we would never have the guts to fight but we proved them wrong, as no doubt the present generation would confound their critics. Please God that they may never be put to the test.

Dom Athanasius was a fine monk and he performed many good works both inside and outside the monastery. As far as I am aware he is still doing so.

BROTHER SEBASTIAN
Lawrence Vernon Alefounder was from a military family with titled connections. His father was a lieutenant-general and his brother was a captain in the 'Blues' so, naturally, Lawrence was destined for the Army. He followed his brother through Rugby and Sandhurst and emerged with a commission in an artillery regiment. He was in hot water with the 'old man' for not getting into a famous regiment. Subsequently, Lawrence was posted as lieutenant in the Indian Army, partly to get away from his father's territory. This was in the famous 17/21st Lancers—more to his father's taste.

Lieutenant Alefounder saw more action than he anti-
cipated, but he acquitted himself with distinction, and was
promoted to captain. Socially, he learnt to play hard and
drink hard. He contracted malaria and was sent to a base
hospital in the hills but otherwise he led a charmed life.
His squadron was recalled to England in 1937 and he
resumed the social round at home.

When war came in 1939, his squadron was sent to a base
in France with the intention of equipping it with light-
armoured cars but when the Germans broke through in
1940 they still had not received their cars. Scouting
parties of German Uhlans were still being used, and Captain Alefounder's troop of horse was ordered to locate them
and report their position.

The armoured scout cars arrived in time to be with-
drawn at Dunkirk. Being in the rear, they escaped via
Calais Harbour. Thus Captain Alefounder finished his
war in a scout car, ultimately joining the Eighth Army
against Rommel, where they were used as a reconnais-
sance force to locate the enemy, radio his position to the
main force and retire before the heavy tanks engaged
them. They were no match for these in armour or fire-
power, only their speed saved them. The Lancers were
frustrated at having to run every time, but this probably
saved Captain Alefounder. Occasionally a scout car would
get caught and blown up but generally they escaped.

On the cessation of German hostilities, the Lancers
were kept in England, for their type of armament was
useless in the jungle against the Japanese.

What moved him to seek admittance to the monastery
after the war nobody knows although his family were
Anglo-Catholic and the menfolk had made retreats at the
abbey. When he arranged his Army discharge, much to the
chagrin of his commanding officer who had recommended
him for promotion and expected him to obtain his majority, he entered the monastery.

The old general, now retired, was also annoyed. His
older son had been killed in action, and his one ewe lamb
was spurning the chance to succeed him on the General
Staff.

Lawrence served postulancy, novitiate and temporary vows and was life professed and ordained, assuming the name Sebastian. He was somewhat peppery in disposition, a relic of Army days and was the terror of the juniors. He once startled them when enquiring of the bursar if the Reverend Mother of a convent had sent the fee she owed him for conducting a retreat. When he was told that it had not arrived, two weeks later, he exploded, "The Bitch!" The abbot who was present raised his eyebrows, the juniors looked up and grinned until he raked them with a glance and the rest looked scandalized with a 'not before the children' sort of expression.

Dom Sebastian suffered repercussions from his malaria and he was allowed the warmth of an open fire in his cell as there was plenty of timber in the community forest land. He felled trees himself for the exercise and sawed them into logs which were stored for his fire. He was appointed workmaster and he worked hard himself beating the youngsters at ploughing the fields. He was also a 'walking Rule' and an excellent example to the juniors. He always kept the silence strictly and if a youngster hung around to say something, he barked, "Get on with it then! If you want to say something, say it and then shut up!"

He was always fair despite his abrupt manner. If anyone broke the Rule, he would reprimand him and then talk to him like a Dutch uncle. His pet aversion was long-haired youths whom he thought were the descendants of Teddy boys when they first appeared at the monastery. When he conversed with them he was amazed that they were from good families and when they were shorn and given the monastic tonsure, they were nice lads. He commented that having made themselves look like women, they found it necessary to assert their masculinity by growing sideburns or beards.

Once, driving the monastery car, I was irritated by the car in front stopping without warning. I muttered unkind words about women drivers as the one in front had hair to the shoulders. Only on passing did I realize that he also had a beard.

My mother maintained that excesses in fashions were a

sign of bad breeding. I shudder to think what she would have made of the present styles, if she were still alive. Dom Sebastian was still more explosive. I was on business at Eton College once when I noticed that long hair had even spread to this bastion of society.

Dom Sebastian was never unjust. Occasionally he would open a window on his own experience, as when a monk confessed to him that he had feelings towards a lady, unworthy of his vows. Dom Sebastian said, "Only one woman ever appealed to me. I met her at my father's house on my rest. If it were not for my vows, I would have left the monastery and asked her to marry me. We are all made the same, laddie. If I can overcome it, so can you. Come and talk about it any time, but in the name of Christ (I mean no profanity) stand by your vows."

The above was told to me by the person concerned. Dom Sebastian's lips were sealed, as it came from the confessional.

After one of his attacks of the 'shivers' as he called them, he would retire to his cell and sleep it off under a pile of blankets before his log fire. On one occasion the infirmarian looked in. It was fortunate that he did as a burning log had fallen off onto the floorboards which were burning merrily. He roused Dom Sebastian and used a fire extinguisher. The maintenance staff replaced the boards and fitted a metal-lined curb.

The following story will illustrate his kindliness. At a certain convent where he said Mass there was a nun who was almost a hundred years old and, although absent-minded, she was in full possession of her faculties. She had been excused offices but she insisted on attending although she was a little confused when the office bell rang and sometimes appeared for meditation when the breakfast bell sounded. Dom Sebastian always made a point of visiting her, curtailing his breakfast time, as she enjoyed a little chat.

On a visit to a central London parish, Dom Sebastian, when crossing a road, stepped straight in front of a car. The car was not speeding, but the driver had no chance of missing him and Dom Sebastian was dead before a passing policeman reached him. There was an inquest and the driver was exonerated.

The news reached the abbot when the police telephoned just before the community went into chapel for compline. There was a delay and the prior led in the community in the abbot's absence. As they stood waiting for the arrival of the abbot, the prior fidgeted with his breviary, wondering whether to start.

The abbot entered, acknowledging the altar mechanically. The community knew from his face that something was wrong. He spoke with a tremor in his voice. "Brethren, I have bad news for you. Dom Sebastian was killed by collision with a car in central London at 2.15 a.m. The police had trouble in tracing his monastery as they contacted the Roman foundations first. They rang me just ten minutes ago. May God rest his soul."

A monk carries no identification papers. His pockets are empty save for a handkerchief and small change for bus fares when out.

The community stood stunned for a few seconds, then the abbot gave the signal to start compline and the cantor for the first time in his life found his voice quaver on the first note.

When the body lay in state before the High Altar, there was not one member of the community, who did not spend some prayer-time beside the coffin.

The funeral, although conducted by the abbot according to monastic rites, could well have been a military one, from the representatives in Army uniform. Dom Sebastian's father, the old general, attended. Although he had never forgiven his son for becoming a monk, he could not let him go to his grave without attending. There were many other Army officers present, whom we did not know. We understood afterwards, that they were representatives of the regiments with which Dom Sebastian had been connected during his military career. This shows his immense popularity, that they should trouble to send representatives considering that Dom Sebastian had long since severed his military connections.

21

The Tri Duum

Holy Week is with us again and with it the most impressive ceremonial of the Church's year, the three days of the Paschal Tri Duum—Maundy Thursday, Good Friday and Holy Saturday—the days of the trial and crucifixion of Our Lord.

I run a great risk of reiterating facts that everyone knows but I explain for the benefit of those who do not. I am no expert on these things but a simple explanation by a very ordinary person may be appreciated, assuming that the reader has no experience of the Catholic faith.

Lent, as all know, commences with Ash Wednesday and finishes forty days later at midnight on the Saturday before Easter Sunday. This is the most sacred time of the year for any Catholic, and the most solemn period of all is the final three days, the ceremonies of which drive home the Passion and Resurrection of Our Lord.

In the monastery on the day before Ash Wednesday the monks present their prepared Lenten Rule to their superior, drawn up by each monk himself, outlining things which he proposes to give up, or extra devotions which he proposes to carry out. The monk has not much left to give up and he is not allowed to abstain from food to the detriment of his health. Therefore his superior will check his Rule carefully. If he smokes, he may give up his meagre ration of tobacco, or he may decide to forgo the sweets and chocolates sent by friends and shared by all.

Inside the monastery, like outside, pancakes are served on Shrove Tuesday. On Ash Wednesday, some of the branches saved from the previous Palm Sunday are burnt and the ashes used at Mass, when the abbot blesses each monk before his fast and imprints a cross of ashes on his forehead—the remaining relic of the custom of dressing in sackcloth and ashes.

During the fast, breakfast is never a cooked meal and a two-course lunch is the only full daily meal. Tea is a cup of tea only and the evening meal is of only one course. Monks are engaged throughout in heavy manual work for five hours a day so a minimum of food is needed to maintain health. During the actual Tri Duum, meals are disorganized by the ceremonies and offices. Any guests in the monastery may have a full tea if they wish it. Once three guests arrived for tea at the usual time, to be told that today tea would be served after the office of none, then at 4.00 p.m. One of the bright lads replied, "Oh, I see. We get afternone tea today!"

There is no recreation hour during Lent. The monks spend the time in their cells in spiritual reading.

On Maundy Thursday, the abbreviated and disrupted office commences with awful gaps left in the morning by the missing vespers. The climax is the evening concelebrated Mass when the abbot washes the feet of twelve of the community, previously notified on the notice-board. This depicts the washing of the disciples' feet by Christ, followed by the solemn re-enactment of the Last Supper.

The great monastery bell is rung for the last time to announce the consecration, as are all the other bells in the monastery in a cacophony of sound. The bells are then silent, the big bell rope tied up, out of reach. The rising bell, office and mealtime bells are replaced by a clapper-board.

The *Tenebrae* or solemn chanting of the offices at matins and lauds heightens the solemnity, with its traditional candles on a triangular holder, one candle being extinguished as each psalm is terminated.

The procession to the altar of repose and the stripping of the altars leaves the monastery dead. The empty tabernacle gapes open and the lights are out. The only sign of life and warmth is at the altar of repose, where the Reserved Sacrament lies. This is a blaze of light and colour, and flowers which have been arriving all day from friends.

Until midnight, two monks will keep vigil while many visitors come to pray.

At midnight the altar of repose becomes the altar of reservation. The candles are extinguished and replaced by a simple altar light. Our communion on Good Friday comes from this Reserved Sacrament after breakfast consisting of tea only. There is no Mass.

After an early "pittance" or snack at 11.30 a.m., a poached egg on toast, washing up is performed hastily so that all can retire to their cells for three hours of prayer, during which time Our Lord hung upon the cross until He died at 3.00 p.m.

Monasteries often possess a splinter of the original cross, gold mounted and authenticated by a Vatican certificate. The veneration of this relic takes place on Good Friday and is a moving sight as monks approach in single file, shoes removed in penance, to kiss this relic of the cross on which our Saviour died.

The subject of relics could have a chapter in its own right. From the Middle Ages, relics were abused and brought into disrepute. Today no relic is considered authentic unless certified by the Vatican who must be satisfied that its claims are valid. The cult is dying.

The Good Friday ceremonies leave one feeling empty. The following Saturday seems interminable—normal working is resumed and there is half an hour of recreation. After recreation, there being no compline, all retire to their beds for the 11.00 p.m. call for the Easter ceremonies, lasting until 1.00 a.m.

The new light is kindled from the brazier outside and the paschal candle is lit, blessed and carried in triumph through the darkened chapel, usually by the most recently ordained deacon. The Light of Christ is announced with the blaze of light from the candles carried by all and the monastery awakes in triumphant symbolism of the Resurrection.

The *Exultet* follows—the solemn announcement of Easter, the blessing of water and the Midnight Mass and renewal of baptismal promises.

After Mass, the matins and lauds of Easter are chanted.

The community then joins the guests for light refreshments, usually getting to bed around 2.30 a.m.

On Easter Monday, the community has a 'lie in'. Early Masses are said at 7.30 a.m. The rest rise in time for prime at 8.00 a.m. After prime, all file in for an informal breakfast. Today is a *dies non* so the menu is a full one—tea or coffee, fruit juice or cereal, boiled eggs, toast and marmalade. The eggs are often tinted or painted. I had not seen this done since my father did it for us at home.

The monks are in a festive mood. The juniors play childish jokes on the seniors, presenting them with a painted pot-egg from the hen run, in order to watch them try to crack it. Childish? Well it makes one feel young again.

Conventual Mass is pontificated, the abbot presiding from his throne in full ceremonial dress, with gloves, staff and gold mitre. After Mass, time is free. Monks walk in groups in the grounds or arrange a swimming party in the nearby river.

Lunch consists of three courses served with table wine, with coffee to follow. After lunch we listen to music on records, our own string quartet or even our own pop group. There is no shortage of 'wags' to recite their party-pieces, encouraged by the community.

After pontifical vespers, tea is served by volunteers in the common-room—plum cake and pastries. After tea, the festivities continue until the evening meal consisting of three courses and coffee, washed down by bottled beer.

Celebrations then continue until time for compline and bed. Usually two more *dies non* and a Long Recreation follow Easter, after which, normal routine returns except that the joyful note of Easter is continued in the office during the following week.

Having touched upon the subject of relics, which is such a sore point with the average Anglican, it would probably not be out of place to say a few words on the subject.

Whilst relics are not esteemed as much in the Anglo-Catholic Church as they are in the Roman Catholic, the Anglo-Catholics accept them as part of the Catholic tradition. Monasteries of my acquaintance do possess authenticated relics, generally of the Holy Cross, which are kept on a special altar and are brought out for veneration on Good Friday.

In the Roman Church, relics are used more frequently. The Vatican certificate of authenticity is only issued for 'first-class' relics, that is for the relic itself. Here the cult of 'second-class' relics has also been accepted. For example, many monasteries hold relics of the bones of saints, duly authenticated. Along comes someone and covers these with a cloth. The cloth is then revered as a second-class relic which, as the French say, *ayant touché* or 'having touched' is then a relic in its own right.

I see no harm in the above if it gives comfort, and provided that the charge of idolatry cannot be levelled.

22

Ambrose and Maurus

BROTHER AMBROSE

John Percival Stapleton was the son of a Lincolnshire farmer. John and his elder brother spent their childhood on a farm and since his brother was only one year his senior, they were inseparable. They ranged over their father's extensive property, sometimes collecting marsh gas from a stream in jam jars by plunging a stick into the mud and releasing the gas into an inverted jam jar full of water, held under the surface. This made a delightful 'pop' when a match was applied to the jar—a trick shown them by their grandfather who lived with them. Under his guidance, they learnt to recognize poisonous berries and follow tracks of foxes and other animals. Here were the tracks of the vixen and cubs, and here the tracks of the dog-fox, ranging from side to side, guarding them from danger.

They were taught to respect birds' nests and to make the mating calls, bringing the birds to them. They learned respect of game coverts and reserves, and were taught how to snare animals for food, without inflicting suffering. They learnt to plough a straight furrow and ride the Shire horses proudly home, inwardly terrified of falling off, until their legs grew long enough to grip the huge backs.

They were educated by a retired clergyman who was a firm believer in practical demonstration and they learnt local geography and biology from specimens collected. This, however, did not prepare them for the entrance examination for a boarding school and as they were also picking up the Lincolnshire dialect from the farm labourers, they were sent to a preparatory school. They were put into separate classes and at first hated it, but they soon settled down. They went on to boarding school and university and both obtained Honours degrees, John in nuclear physics and his brother in pharmacy.

John went to work at Windscale and first contacted the monastery via his church. He entered as a postulant, and eventually found himself in life vows and priested, at which stage we meet him.

He had a pleasant disposition and was much sought after to conduct retreats. When the Second World War broke out he was not called up of course but his brother served in the R.A.M.C. at a base hospital in Singapore where he was taken prisoner by the Japanese and eventually succumbed to brutal treatment and food shortage. This was a severe blow to Dom Ambrose, as he was now called, but he found the grace to forgive his enemies.

Later, becoming a car driver, he was out with the abbot one day when they realized that the door was not closed properly. The abbot said it would have been awkward if he had fallen out as people might have said that Dom Ambrose had pushed him. Without batting an eyelid, Dom Ambrose replied that it would indeed have been awkward as he would have had to shut the door himself.

He complained about the vestments. Being small, the same chasuble which reached the floor on him, looked like an oversized dicky on the tallest priest.

At fifty-five, his retreat work came to an abrupt end when he suffered a coronary thrombosis. He was at the local railway station and was found hanging onto the fence in the agony of cardiac infarction. The ambulance was called and he was rushed into the intensive care unit. After six weeks he was brought home to the monastery and put to bed under the care of the infirmarian and the monastery doctor, who tended him tirelessly. The community gave up their recreation time to sit with him. At last he could have his habit put on and be wheeled into chapel for Mass and a breath of air.

The abbot gave him the job of monitoring the radio for news and instructed him to make a library of classical music on tape, from his bed. He was presented with more sophisticated equipment, hence the excellent tape library at his monastery.

He lived three years under these irksome conditions before this state of affairs came to an abrupt end. The infirmarian was awoken in the night by his bell ringing and, knowing that Dom Ambrose would not trouble him unnecessarily, he hurried to him. He found him in the throes of a second coronary and immediately telephoned for an ambulance, which had arrived by the time they had carried him downstairs on a stretcher. The abbot went to hospital with him and administered the Last Rites on the way. He died on arrival at the hospital.

His body was dressed in his priestly robes and laid in state before the altar. The funeral took place without relatives as he was now alone in the world. Only the community mourned him and he was laid to rest within the monastery, beside his departed brethren. A plain cross of opepe wood was made and engraved by the workshop and planted at his head.

BROTHER MAURUS

Robert Nelson Browning claimed that he was descended from two famous families—his mother's side had produced the famous admiral and his father's side the famous poet. He first became aware of monasticism at the age of twelve when, on holiday with his family in Devonshire, he was taken to see Buckfast Abbey under construction. He and his father were taken round, and the boy was greatly impressed.

Being a boy, he was also impressed with the Devonshire cream tea which followed. Trestle tables were laid under the cover of outbuildings in the tea-gardens in Buckfast-leigh. There were large bowls of clotted cream and strawberry jam, with plates of bread and butter. Waitresses brought round tea and replenished the food. One paid a shilling to enter and eat one's fill and Robert had to be restrained from over-indulgence.

At eighteen, just prior to entering university, he returned with his friend, on a walking holiday. The tea-gardens were the same, except for the price which was now half a crown. The monastery buildings had been completed and the pair were so impressed that they enquired about entry to the Roman foundation. However, since both were Anglo-Catholics, the superior said that they would have to transfer to the Roman Catholic Church and anyway, he could not accept them immediately. They must return home and consider it. He also advised them to complete their university courses first.

Somewhat rebuffed, Robert went home to the same advice from his father so he reluctantly entered the university. He came down with an Honours degree as expected and his monastic aspirations seemed to have faded.

He invited a female student to the house to meet his parents. The family were not impressed with the girl but they wisely kept silent, hoping the affair would fade out as others had done. However, immediately Robert was settled in a job and had collected a little capital, he announced that he was going to marry the girl and the wedding took place in June 1939.

When the war started in September, Robert volunteered for air crew in the R.A.F. and left for Cranwell. After a pathetically short training period, he came out with his pilot's wings and the rank of Pilot Officer. He was at home for fourteen days' leave prior to drafting. He had set up a nice home and he and his wife spent the leave in an atmosphere of forced gaiety, entering the social whirl which disguised one's feelings in those dark days. Two days before his leave ended, his drafting papers came. He was to report to a transit unit for shipment to the United States as an instructor. He knew he had passed well, but had not expected this.

The Americans were not at war then, but were stretching neutrality to its limits in Great Britain's favour (and, incidentally, pocketing the huge benefits raised by the mortgaging of our colonies for their help). The United States provided the airfields and Great Britain provided the planes and instructors. Robert knew his wife could not accompany him and, in any case, she was expecting a baby.

When the child was born, Robert's wife left their home

and went back to her parents but immediately after she moved in, her father suffered a stroke and died. When his will was read, Robert's wife was the sole beneficiary provided that she left her mother a stated annuity—in this way double death duties were avoided.

Robert's wife found herself a comparatively rich woman and this seems to have affected her behaviour. She left home, leaving the boy with her mother, and re-entered the social whirl at the officers' club. She went about a lot with a brother officer of Robert's, the family knew of this but kept it from Robert as they hoped that it would come to an end before his return.

Robert was sent home unexpectedly in the winter of 1944, to be confronted with his wife's demand for a divorce. He refused to divorce her because of his religious beliefs but they separated.

Robert's problems were not improved by the untimely death of his father. He regained possession of his house and his widowed mother kept house for him, after he had been refused admittance to the monastery. He got his old job back and became an oblate of the abbey.

One evening, three years later, Robert answered the door to be presented with his wife's divorce papers. She was divorcing him for technical desertion as the necessary three years apart had elapsed. The divorce went through undefended. The day after the decree absolute, his wife married the other officer, in spite of her earlier protests, when questioned by Robert's solicitors, that there was nothing between them.

Robert, though now free of marital ties, could not leave his mother on her own. The abbot agreed to let him enter as a postulant, but was prepared to wait until after Robert's mother died. In the event, this was only a matter of two years. Robert had done his duty by her.

He entered as a postulant at an advanced age to find himself junior to men half his age. He took this in his stride but, being used to management, it irked him to take orders from youngsters when experience told him that they were wrong, however he accepted the situation.

The position was a little easier when he entered temporary vows and left the junior common-room. Earlier he had encountered the obnoxious lay brother mentioned before, who inflicted all the humiliations on Brother Maurus which he could devise. Brother Maurus was astounded that this could happen in the House of God but he had been warned that the world could not be kept out of the monastery.

Dom Maurus was disturbed by the disintegration of the liturgy and the words Series Two assumed a distasteful significance. When he was life professed, the ceremony was in English instead of the Latin of his temporary profession.

The translation of the office into English led to strange situations. Opening the Benedictus Antiphon for All Saints of our Order, the hebdomadary led the choir in with "You who have followed me, shall receive an hundred-fold. . . ." He realized the trap but could do nothing to avoid it and he came out with an unmusical "Yoo hoo". There was a pause whilst the choir tried to smother its mirth. The original Latin is harmless, *"Vos qui reliquistis omnia et seculi estis me centuplum accipietis. . . ."* But, I suppose one must be fair and say that the Latin text can also offend. One of the Advent antiphone starts *"Ante me . . ."* that is "Before me . . .", which was rendered as "Auntie May" I rather imagine with malice aforethought.

Before life profession, Brother Maurus was not directly involved in the chapter squabbles over the liturgy. Having been elected for life profession he had a discussion with the Confessor Extraordinary about the problems involved and eventually went to London to see the Bishop Visitor and then to the palace of the bishop of the diocese. He evidently passed muster as he was allowed to go forward.

After life profession and gaining a seat in chapter, he realized how far the disruption of the liturgy had gone. He also found who the real culprits were. There were three factions: the traditionalists who wanted things left alone, but were prepared to compromise to the extent of translation into English; the modernists who wanted the whole thing altered and the remainder who would accept anything for a quiet life. Unfortunately, the latter would vote as suggested by the abbot, which would mean that the traditionalists would be outvoted.

Dom Maurus was studying for ordination when the final blow happened. The new novice master invited groups of university students to give 'pop' concerts. These were given in chapel where men and girls entered the sanctuary. Dom Maurus spoke to one of the senior traditionalists who tried his utmost to stop this, but to no avail. Protests to the abbot and the diocesan bishop were unavailing.

Dom Maurus went on his annual rest and thus secured time to think upon it. On his return, he consulted with the abbot who remained obdurate—he was not prepared to prevent further disruptions. Dom Maurus therefore applied for secularization—a decision that was not taken lightly. On life profession, a monk abandons material possessions, money, property and shareholdings and there is no guarantee that they will be refunded on secularization. The decision rests with the Archbishop of Canterbury. In the event, Dom Maurus received back bank-balance, property and shareholdings, insofar as they could be re-converted.

It took the best part of a year to arrange the formalities. Dom Maurus was notified to vacate his seat in chapter during these discussions and allowed to go for an interview with his old company for a job. Latterly he was confined to his cell and had his meals brought to him. He read more books during this period than ever before or since.

He had a personal problem in that his monastic tonsure was growing out and looked as if the mice had been at it—it caused curious glances when he left.

The day of departure arrived and he felt as if he were suffering from the plague, as he was left completely alone except for one senior who came rather furtively to bid him farewell and help him with his cases. An old friend and his wife fetched him home in their car and Dom Maurus bought them all a meal on the motorway from the one hundred pounds advanced by the bursar, against the return of his money. Thus he emerged into the world to make a fresh start.

After the statutory six months, Dom Maurus received his secularization papers from the Archbishop of Canterbury, with a personal letter. The Reverend Dom Maurus, O.S.B. became Mr R. N. Browning, B.Sc. once again. Shortly afterwards he met a female friend. Later they married and their marriage was an extremely happy one, I am pleased to report.

23

Golden Jubilee and Other Celebrations

Religious institutions, in common with those outside the monastery, celebrate the jubilees of the date of their foundation when there is great rejoicing, with Masses of thanksgiving. Individuals also celebrate the anniversaries of their life profession and ordination. Monasteries have their own priests to officiate but convents have to import them from outside.

A certain convent had a Golden Jubilee and requested a monastery some hundred miles away to supply priests and altar party for Mass. The party set out before 7.00 a.m. by car hoping to arrive for Mass by 11.00 a.m. There were two cars containing nine monks including the abbot who was celebrating. The car boots were full of vestments and equipment.

The first hour and a half went well and they made good time but then disaster struck. They arrived in the urban area of a large town in the morning commuter rush and only managed ten miles an hour through the town. Once on the motorway, traffic thinned and the drivers realized they would have to hurry. The driver in the car carrying the abbot, asked him to keep his eyes off the speedometer as monastery drivers have strict instructions always to observe speed limits.

After leaving the motorway, there was less traffic and they quickly reached the lanes leading to the convent. Here they had planned to have a coffee break and, indeed, the flasks were passed round, but the drivers resolutely refused to stop. One of the monks spilt his coffee into his lap but, despite his protests that he was scalding to death, the driver told him uncompromisingly to flap his habit out of the window to dry it as he was not stopping. The monk spent an uncomfortable day explaining away the wet patch on the front of his habit.

At last the party arrived at the convent, with just five minutes in hand to accomplish half an hour's preparation. However the Mass started only five minutes late.

After Mass, everyone was led into the *statio* for an excellent glass of sherry, then into the refectory for lunch. When the community was founded, the refectory was built for over 100 nuns, at this celebration, something like 130 sat down for lunch which was a four-course meal. Nuns are renowned for their cooking and this time they had excelled themselves. Champagne was served with the meal and for the speeches.

Our abbot proposed the health and prosperity of the community and one of the nuns proposed the health of the abbess, who replied to both. The senior sister proposed the health of the community and one of our monks replied. Their novice mistress introduced and proposed the health of their latest (and only) novice, who replied. There were votes of thanks for the help of their oblates and helpers, who had made the meal possible.

All the speeches were full of fun and witticisms which would bear repeating except for the risk of boring the reader. The oblates were responsible for the decoration of the tables and the floral arrangements were superb. They also served the meal so that the nuns could all join in. Coffee was served afterwards in the common-room and guests and community were able to circulate and converse.

After seeking out the abbess to congratulate her on the success of the occasion, three of our monks got into conversation with a female oblate. She was a local schoolteacher on holiday and was an enthusiastic motorist. She had never visited our monastery and was promptly invited. She enquired if they had ever seen the local beauty-spot called 'Bluebell Woods', as she had been there only days ago and they were at their best. Would the monks care to see it? She would take them in the car and as it was only five miles it would not take long.

The monks said they would love to, but could not go without the abbot's permission. The lady said she would soon fix that. She cornered the abbot, and seeing him nod, they were away. The woods more than justified her enthusiasm—a carpet of blue.

On the way back, she said that it was a pity that vespers with celebrant had not been laid on and asked them if they would oblige. They said they would if the abbot gave his permission. She said nothing more, but consulted the abbess and then tackled the abbot suggesting that he could leave the small car for the three to return in. They would be back for compline and the others could easily squash into the large car. The abbot was rather amused. He said all arrangements seemed to have been made. Could she tell him when he might get his monks back? Unabashed, she said she would give them tea after vespers and see that they were away by five o'clock. The abbot said afterwards, his was the only monastery with a lady abbot.

The topic of celebrations brings to mind a community of Roman nuns who invited a party of Anglican monks to join them in their rejoicings over one of their community who had been canonized by the Pope. The High Mass was celebrated by their own priests and the Anglicans had special permission to communicate. Their nun, who had been dead for the prescribed number of years, had lived a very holy life and miracles had been attributed to her intervention both at home and in the mission field and some were said to have happened after her death.

The question of miracles is rather a vexed one. The Anglican Low Church dismisses them as 'popery' and the High Church evades the issue. Whatever one's view, some miracles may be dismissed as a figment of the imagination while others are 'not proven'. There still remains a hard core which undoubtedly took place and have no rational explanation. These must be accepted. Coincidence? Maybe, but what about the healings at Lourdes?

After Mass there was a buffet meal and one had the opportunity of talking with "the other side". One then realizes that we are not always right, just as the Romans are not always wrong. One of the nuns remarked that it was a spiritual uplift to see Anglicans taking communion beside them. She regretted that we could not celebrate Mass in her convent and hoped fervently that this would soon be rectified.

Monks are often sent out to celebrate a jubilee of a nun's profession. Sometimes a large contingent goes then the full S.A.T.B. version can be rendered, and the music is most inspiring.

There is liaison between monasteries and convents across the denominational barrier and the nuns often undertake such tasks as the renovation of vestments. I can remember going out to rebuild the altar of a convent (I nearly said to alter their altar). The job took two of us more than a week but it was quite enjoyable and we had meals and said office with them.

On many occasions we made and fitted new choir stalls, paschal candles and crucifixes for convents and also refectory tables and other furniture.

It is not unknown for the good nuns to ring up and ask for assistance with such things as burst water-mains or erecting tents for a garden-party. All part of the service! In return, they offer help in darning and mending and other things requiring the female touch. One community always used to supply two or three huge pumpkins which were about two feet across.

As with the vexed question of relics, the veneration of the saints is not regarded as seriously by the Anglo-Catholics as it is by the Roman Catholics. We revere the saints sufficiently to esteem it an honour to take the name of one when noviced, but the Anglo-Catholic Church generally does not pay them the same reverence as the Roman Church. Certainly our church does not canonize them.

With regard to miracles, we are somewhat closer, as many Anglicans, both High and Low Church, send their sick to places like Lourdes for prayers to be offered in the hope of a miracle of healing. We have our own shrine in this country at Walsingham, where miracles are said to have taken place. There is no doubt that some happenings must be regarded as miraculous.

24

The Monastic Year

CHRISTMAS IN THE MONASTERY

Most people visualize Christmas in the monastery as a very sorry affair but in fact nothing is further from the truth. True, we have the Advent fast first, but for several weeks beforehand, the caterer saves up and puts aside extras for the feast, as the housewife does at home. Kitchen staff are reinforced by helpers to prepare mince pies, Christmas pudding and cake. A large box is placed in the hall for the collection of sweet chestnuts, which the monks gather from our trees in their spare time, for roasting and stuffing.

Presents of Christmas fare begin to arrive from friends—cigars, cigarettes, bottles of wine and spirits and eatables. Monks pool all their consumable presents.

The week before Christmas, the great or 'O' antiphons appear in the liturgy and a squad of monks go out into the woods to select and fell trees to supply the logs for the great open fireplace in the common-room, which is kept burning over Christmas.

On Christmas Eve after compline, which is earlier than usual, the monks rest on their beds until the bell tolls at 11.00 p.m. for the start of the celebrations when Christmas matins, Midnight Mass and lauds are sung. Afterwards there is a late buffet snack and we retire to bed after 2.00 a.m.

Some of us are sent out to assist in the Midnight Mass in one of the nearby parishes. I well remember being fetched in a churchwarden's car and being returned to the monastery in the early hours, after a long journey, sliding about in deep snow, with shovel at the ready to dig out.

On Christmas Day, we are allowed a lie-in until 6.30 a.m. for prime at 7.00 a.m., followed by Low Masses and breakfast at 8.00 a.m. Breakfast, which is a 'talking' meal taken together as a family consists of grapefruit, boiled ham, bread, butter, marmalade and tea or coffee.

During the Christmas period, no unnecessary work is done and all help with cooking and table chores. Generally, there are no guests at Christmas but any remaining ones help with the work and are integrated with the community at meals. All have a card with their name on it and these are shuffled at each meal and placed on the table at random so that no one knows with whom he will be sitting.

At 10.00 a.m. comes the Christmas Pontifical Mass. The scene glitters with vestments and gold plate. After Mass, dinner is prepared and after sext and none sherry is served before the roaring log fire, which gives a cosy feeling to the whole building.

At 1.00 p.m. dinner is served—turkey soup, roast turkey with all its trimmings, plum pudding with rum sauce, hot mince pies, with a couple of glasses of dinner wine and nuts, fruit and coffee.

After dinner all wash up and retire to the senior common-room for the Queen's speech on the radio. A short walk is often taken and at 3.45 p.m. the office of vespers takes place, also pontificated, followed by tea served by volunteers in the common-room consisting of cake, mince pies, pastries and tea. The evening is spent in the common-room, lit by candles, singing carols and secular songs around the piano. Each monk is expected to contribute his party-piece greeted by cheers or groans according to its antiquity. It is all taken in good part.

At 7.00 p.m. supper of pork pie, mince pies, cheese, biscuits and bottled beer is served. After washing up the monks retire to the common-room for a request programme of music on the music centre. Sweets, chocolates, nuts and fruit are available. At 8.30 p.m. comes compline and bed, which all are ready for, having been up most of the previous night.

On Boxing Day, we arise at 6.15 a.m. for matins and lauds. Offices are normal today. The day is free as yesterday, and the abbot, prior and monastery officers do all the essential cooking and washing up. The next day is also a holiday, but on 29th December we return to normal, until the Epiphany when two more holidays are observed as above.

During the season, we usually meet with neighbouring convents and monasteries, when we visit them or entertain them for tea or have combined vespers. The local church and handbell ringers sometimes give us a concert, a concert pianist gives a recital or an operatic society gives a show.

The snow one Christmas was deep and the monks went walking in improvised snow attire, looking like Arctic explorers. The habit is useless in snow. I saw the tracks of a vixen and followed them to thick undergrowth, I remembered that foxes can be savage if cornered and withdrew as I did not wish to surprise her.

During Christmas, a party of visiting nuns included a newly clothed novice. On her previous visit she had been a postulant in civilian clothing. I was chatting with her when up came our novice master and said, "Congratulations, Sister! This is the first time I have seen you in your clothes!" I choked into my coffee cup. The novice master looked uncomfortable, opened his mouth to speak, then shut it again. The nun was highly amused by his embarrassment.

Monks at most monasteries are not permitted to take their annual rest during the Christmas period. Christmas is reckoned to be a period when everybody should be at home and the spiritual home of the monk is his monastery.

A monk often receives the sympathies of friends who know that he will be in the monastery during the Christmas period, under the mistaken idea that he will miss all the festivities and live on bread and water. I can assure you that there is as much fun and festivity within the monastery as there is outside it, if not more, and I trust that the above narrative will dispel any erroneous ideas on the subject.

FOUR SEASONS IN THE MONASTERY
Other chapters have described the impact upon the monastery of the personalities of the monks; this chapter describes the impact upon the monk of his monastery. Occurrences, which would pass without comment in the outside world, assume a greater significance when reflected upon in solitude, with all the time in the world, in the monastery.

The descriptions have been gleaned in the course of conversation with monks and are therefore reproduced in the first person, as they were received.

Spring
I noticed that the sun came through by midday today, making its presence felt. The snowdrops and crocuses are out in abundance under the trees, announcing the arrival of spring. As yet, there is not much power in the sun and I am pleased to wear my cloak whilst walking in the monastery grounds.

The notice-board had the usual request up this morning, asking us to name the dates which we would prefer for our annual rest. This does not mean we shall all get the dates for which we ask, unless we happen to have sufficient seniority to be given our first choice.

Nature re-awakens with every day that passes. The catkins are all in flower and I see many fresh trees showing indisputable evidence of new bud growth. Two domestic cats from one of the farms nearby have adopted us and set up home together in our open-fronted barn. They have made a bed in a dark corner in the straw. The tom-cat is a large black animal and spends most of his time hunting for rodents amongst the shrubs. The female is almost pure white, and spends all her time in the straw. She spat at me and showed signs of fury when I tried to investigate this morning so I could not see if the family had arrived yet. It would take a much more intrepid investigator than I to approach more closely. It will be interesting to see what the kittens look like, with one parent pure black and the other pure white.

The blackbirds are busily staking out their territory, and the cock birds are fighting one another over it. The woodpeckers are hammering away at the trees, and I spotted one beautifully coloured bird clinging to the side of a tree. The dawn chorus of birds was very persistent this morning, when we came out of matins and lauds.

I notice that the brethren who look after the gardens are showing signs of spring activity. Mowers are being overhauled and greased and the workshop brethren are being waylaid to loan tools and supply nuts and bolts.

We appear to have been invaded by a family of Japanese deer. When I first saw one in the early morning I thought it was a greyhound. It walked out of the bushes and across the top of the lawn. It vanished into the bushes again and I wondered if someone had lost a greyhound. The next sighting was closer and I saw the whole family—parents and a young one. This time there was no doubt that they were deer, but so small that one would doubt the evidence of one's eyes.

That evening at recreation, one monk said that he had read in a magazine that there were Japanese deer breeding in the wild in southern England. It seems that some had escaped from a private estate.

We were all delighted and hoped that they would stay with us. We even discussed their diet with the idea of providing food for them. We soon found out what their diet was. One of the monks had a sunken garden which he had cultivated and stocked himself in his spare time. He found the deer feeding on his favourite plants and immediately gave chase, joined by two other monks. The deer leapt through the undergrowth with the monks in pursuit. Whether they went to ground on our property, or whether they left for good, no one knows, but from that time, they were never seen again.

Then the arguments started. The gardeners were not pleased, as they had lost many seedlings. The rest cried shame, saying that it was worth the loss of a bit of foodstuff to have such graceful creatures about the place. It was a nine days' wonder. Even guests wrote to the guestmaster enquiring after them.

The buds burst so quickly this year that I was too late to notice if the oak or the ash came out first, so I am still wondering if we shall have a soak or a splash this year, according to the old rhyme.

Grey squirrels are performing their acrobatics in the treetops again, and nibbling away at the tender new leaves. These they bite off and let drop to the ground, giving the appearance of a false leaf fall.

We have been plagued for several evenings by some schoolboys who ought to be old enough to know better. They come through or under the boundary fences, ring the visitor's doorbell and run away, much to the annoyance of the elderly lay brother who acts as porter. They also tap on the windows of the ground-floor cells whilst the occupants are at study.

On being chased away, they climbed the high monastery boundary wall, which runs down one side of the grounds, and ran along its flat top. Our porter nearly had a fit, as it is all of twelve feet high in places and he was afraid of them falling.

One must admit that they have some initiative anyway. They must have walked from the village, which is more than we do unless we have to. I suppose it is a holiday for them and they get bored as we did when we were boys.

We used to go into parts of the town where the front doors opened on to the pavement, tie the two doorknobs together with string, and, knocking on both doors, we would retire to await developments. One must remember one's own misdeeds before condemning the youth of today.

Summer
The house martins are with us again. They have built nests under the eaves for many years now and they seem to

occupy the same nests each year, repairing them as needed. It is wonderful to watch them collecting mud in their beaks and mixing it with saliva before spitting it out in the form of a cement. The finished construction is marvellous when seen close up. I had a chance to examine a nest when I was up a ladder doing repairs. It is marvellous when one thinks that it was made using only the bird's beak.

All through the summer, we have visiting monks from other monasteries staying with us. Today, a non-Christian monk arrived from Thailand—a Buddhist. The usual courtesies were extended to him, of course and we were surprised when he accepted the offered seat in choir.

His English is surprisingly good, and we found him quite charming in conversation at recreation. I know a little of the Buddhist faith from my studies of comparative religions but I was pleased to learn more. The Buddhist monk takes no vows of stability. In Buddhist countries, all the male population always spend part of their lives as monks, when their education is complete and before they settle down to married life.

Apparently, the Buddhist admits of no personal God, no Saviour, no helper. He stands alone. There appears to be no prayer life as we know it, since he has no one to pray to. Instead they spend hours each day in meditation, through which they seek peace and tranquillity. The Buddhist moral philosophy is the same as ours in that one's neighbour is placed before oneself. The Buddhist believes there are three primary corruptions, 'desire, existence and ignorance', and giving in to these results in rebirth into a lower state than man. I can accept his repugnance of desire and ignorance but fail to see why mere existence is considered a sin. Attaining perfection will result in rebirth into a higher state each time, until he eventually accomplishes 'Nirvana' or fusion with the supreme being. (God?)

The visiting Buddhist monk was fascinated with our faith and would accept Christ as a major prophet, but not as God. I would have liked to have had his candid opinion of us, but he was careful not to say anything derogatory, and, of course, we observed the same convention.

179

Speaking of visiting monks and clergy reminds me of the Patriarch of Romania, who visited us when I was a novice, along with his monks and clergy. It was a memorable day. We practised a song of welcome in Romanian of all things. Music and verse were provided by the Romanian Embassy in London and we rehearsed it carefully, only to be told at the last minute that it would not do at all. We had rehearsed it as we would sing it ourselves, but we were told that Romanians deliver it with the full power of the lungs. We wondered if we were being teased until the day arrived. When we started, the visitors soon recognized it and joined with great gusto, nearly raising the roof.

The patriarch presented each one of us with a small picture of Christ in Glory, painted and framed by his own nuns. I still have mine by me. He also presented the community with an icon and attendant hanging sanctuary lamp. One of our monks who received the present thought it was for him, owing to the language difficulty, but he was soon disillusioned.

We met the party over refreshments on the lawn before they departed. For once the English summer behaved itself. The meeting was not as satisfactory as it might have been since the patriarch was the only one who spoke any English and that with much misunderstanding, and none of our party spoke any Romanian. We managed some conversation in French but the dialogue was mostly conducted in sign language with much smiling and bobbing of heads.

The season of annual rests has started. This leaves manpower somewhat depleted and we find ourselves having to do two jobs. Most of our visitors arrive at this time of the year also, thus we find ourselves doubly extended. They, of course, invade our shop and empty it of our hand-made goods which then have to be replaced. However, I must not appear to complain, as the shop profits help us to keep going.

We are delighted to receive visitors, particularly one annual visit of disabled visitors who come in their specially equipped coach without seats but adapted to take them in their wheelchairs. They have a hydraulic lift and the chairs are loaded and strapped in position.

We usually provide lunch and tea and they enjoy attending vespers, after which the monks take them for a walk around the monastery grounds, workshops and farm. Chairs occasionally get bogged down in the mud but there are many willing hands to hoist them out.

This year a particularly jovial priest came along with them. He had a fund of funny stories, from which he kept up a running commentary as we went. One I can remember.

A priest had just celebrated his fiftieth year of ordination when he died. When he reached the gates of heaven, Peter was reluctant to let him in. During the delay, a young woman in a mini-skirt, the fashion of the day, walked up and was admitted immediately. When the priest complained that she had gone in immediately, whilst he was kept waiting outside, Peter explained that she was a learner driver and had put the fear of the Lord into more people in a single day than the priest had in the whole of his fifty years' ministry.

The sun is getting very hot now, and we welcome the chance of doing a little sunbathing during our one-hour midday siesta. We have a clearing in the woods which is euphemistically called 'the Monks' Garden'. All paths through the woods leading to it are marked 'Private', so that we get a chance there to relax free from the interference of visitors.

Most visitors do honour the signs but some seem to think that they apply to everyone but themselves. The lady who wandered into the Monks' Garden and found several monks lying in the sun without their habits, clad in a very brief pair of underpants, had only herself to blame. She did however try to register a complaint.

The garden shed in the Monks' Garden is used to store deck-chairs. They are in great demand during hot weather. One appreciates the one-hour siesta in the middle of the day, particularly when the weather is hot and after being up since 5.00 a.m. We often remember that we owe this peculiarly Italian custom (shared with other hot climates) to our founder St Benedict, who was an Italian.

The hot sun makes us realize that those who were allocated an early rest this year, had rather a thin time weatherwise. Those who went later caught the sun, and thanked their lucky stars.

Our Corpus Christi procession this year was worth putting on record.

It was right in the middle of the wet period, and the day started with pouring rain. The cars and coaches came in, and those of us with indoor jobs sympathized with those allocated the duty of car-park attendants. These poor souls were wading in pools of water as they directed the vehicles.

The people came in looking wet and bedraggled, but fortunately only about two hundred turned up in place of the usual four hundred or more. As they came in, we packed them into the guest reception area, which is designed to accommodate about sixty, comfortably seated. We relieved them of their wet coats and ushered them on to the first and second floors of the monastery, which we had cleared for the purpose.

Only the altar party and visiting clergy processed. The remaining visitors were packed in the chapel for the ceremony. The bit of crowd control performed by the monks would have done credit to the police force.

It was a work of art, swinging a censer in the confined space of the corridors used for the procession, packed as they were with visitors. The people in the chapel sang lustily however, and apparently the arrangements were satisfactory, judging from the comments at tea-time.

Tea, usually served on the lawns, had to be split up into four different areas indoors, the monks doing yeoman service, keeping the visitors supplied with urns of tea, pastries and sausage rolls. The Tannoy system was used to keep everybody informed and to make special announcements.

Invariably, it was found that when one area was overfull

182

and we wished to guide people into another area, that somebody's little 'Tommy' was already ahead of his family and had to be hooked back, usually clutching a sausage roll in one hand and a sticky cake in the other.

After tea, everybody voted it the best ever Corpus Christi, since they had been allowed, by force of circumstances, to visit areas of the monastery into which they would never have gone otherwise.

Autumn
The first signs of autumn are with us. Our migratory birds are gathering for the mass exodus. The swallows and martins have already gone. They seem to know better than man when the cold weather is coming and remove themselves in very good time, before it arrives.

Now the warmth of summer is over, we find ourselves providing free meals for increasing numbers of 'wayfarers' or tramps. Personally, I question if this is necessary in today's Welfare State and wonder how many rogues we harbour. It is, however, laid down in our Rule and was no doubt a very desirable service when St Benedict wrote the Rule. I would suggest however, that some modification is made to conform to present-day conditions. We know we do harbour some rogues, from the questions asked by the police who call regularly, also from the rapid disappearance of some of the wayfarers when the police arrive. I have come across several Irish labourers who are working nearby on the motorway; they earn a great deal of money and spend it all on drink in the village pub. There they make a nuisance of themselves, often becoming extremely drunk. They usually sober up in a hedge row somewhere and then come to us for a free meal.

I suppose that it is inevitable that anyone performing any charitable work will occasionally be deceived but probably the odd deserving case is worth all the others— the point is debatable.

The mornings are getting darker now, but nature throws in a consolation prize in the form of the lovely autumn tints. The delicious marmalade tint of the oak trees, and the darker gold of the chestnuts, set against the dark green of the conifers. I counted six different shades of green, looking out of my cell window.

Driving the monastery car for the 'convent run', that is delivering two pairs of brethren to say Mass at local convents within a five-mile radius of the monastery, we see the world awakening. It is still dark, and rabbits, stoats and other small quadrupeds scuttle out of the beams of the headlights as we sweep through the narrow country lanes. A blackbird swoops away from us, scolding us angrily for disturbing his morning peace. A small group of workmen stand at the bus-stop as we approach the village. We turn into the first convent drive, deposit the priest and server at the convent entrance, do a quick three-point turn and drive out again quickly.

After the last convent has been visited, the first streaks of daylight are visible in the east. In the far distance, bright patches of light indicate towns, and further away, a strip of bright lights indicate the local airport runway. The stars fade and mingle with the navigation lights of one or two planes, circling to land on the airport runway. I expect that they will be pleased to land and get their breakfast, unless they had it earlier in the air.

Lights begin to show in the houses scattered along the lanes. The village awakes as we pass through it. The little butcher's shop is a blaze of light as they take in a delivery of fresh meat from the refrigerated van standing outside.

A police patrol car is parked in a quiet backwater. They wave as we pass, recognizing the monastery car, not much for them to do here—probably stopped for a quiet smoke, all the same, better not to tempt providence—we will observe the speed limit strictly whilst within the village area. He may fall in behind us if we depart too quickly.

We turn into the monastery grounds, park the car and hurry into the refectory for breakfast. We are just in time to eat it hurriedly and go into prime at 8.00 a.m. followed by spiritual reading. Then we must hurry out to fetch the two altar parties from the convents. The nuns will have given them their breakfast, after Mass. We have to bring them home in time for conventual Mass in the monastery.

It is broad daylight now. Everything has woken up and come to life since the first trip. Near the village we meet the string of early morning commuters, awaiting their turn to enter the motorway slip road on their way to work in the nearest town. Ten years ago, this was a quiet lane with scarcely a car to be seen.

Entering the first convent drive, we give a couple of 'toots' on the horn and out they come, the priest clutching a letter from the Reverend Mother to be delivered to the next convent.

Whipping through narrow lanes, a blackbird flew straight into us with a thud. He bounced off and lay still. A cyclist coming in the opposite direction stopped and picked him up, then waved us on, throwing him into the ditch. I had stopped in case he was not dead. I hate killing such a bird, even accidentally. The blackbird is such a lovely bird, mating as he does for life, which is unusual in the world of nature.

Collecting from the next convent and leaving the letter, we turned for home.

The wind yesterday has nearly cleared the leaves from the trees, except for the oaks. These even, have lost their rich marmalade colour and are looking dowdy. I can see the birds and grey squirrels now, darting about on the upper branches. It is said that the grey squirrel has killed off the native brown variety. I think it is only that they have taken over the food supplies by virtue of numbers and the red variety has gone elsewhere. The grey squirrel reproduces much more rapidly than the original red squirrel. The Government offer five pence for each grey squirrel's tail, as they are such a destructive pest, and we help in the culling operation with our one and only shotgun, otherwise they multiply much too quickly. This is a pity as they are pretty little creatures, although some people tell us that they are only tree rats.

All members of the religious orders, men and women, give the same answer, when asked what is the main bone of contention in the monastery or convent. They all reply "windows".

It appears that there are two schools of thought regarding windows. Some think that they should be kept open all the time for ventilation. Others think that they should be kept closed all the time to prevent draughts.

In the former category is the 'cold air fiend' who thinks that the inside temperature should be reduced to that of the outside air. In the latter category is the 'fug fiend' who thinks that all windows should be permanently kept closed, until it is uncomfortably hot and stuffy inside.

Myself, I like a reasonable compromise. I like fresh air but not cold air and I hate draughts, since in a draught, I quickly develop a stiff neck or shoulder.

The situation is bad enough outside the monastery, but it is possible to depart from an atmosphere that one does not like, or remove oneself from a draught. In the monastery, one is compelled to endure it. If one is given a seat near an open window, one is in trouble if a cold air fiend is encountered. A stuffy atmosphere likewise, is unpleasant but one must endure it if confronted with a fug fiend.

This state of affairs always produces friction and in this instance, the usual monastic charitableness or consideration for others seems to be completely non-existent. The situation is perhaps the chief single cause of disruption in the monastery.

When the central heating is turned on, relief comes, in that the windows must be kept closed, by order, to prevent loss of heat and economize on fuel. Until that time, the battle rages between the advocates of fresh air and the sufferers from stiff necks and frozen shoulders.

The late November sky in the early morning. The dense blackness of the sky just before dawn. The waning moon, half gone, with streaky clouds scudding by. If one observes it, the clouds seem to stand still whilst the moon races past.

As I came out of the night office, I thought that this was worth getting up to see, if nothing else. The stars peep through the gaps in the clouds. The Plough over there near the horizon is the only complete constellation which one can see through the gaps in the clouds.

The drone of an aeroplane overhead. The clouds jostle one another like a lot of rush hour commuters.

The smell of dampness in the air—not the summer freshness, but a dank dampness, which presses down upon one. The wet flagstones of the monastery path. Winter is fast approaching.

Yesterday, as we left vespers, the sky to the west was the colour of burnished brass, so that we should have a fine day today, if the old adage is true.

The nights get longer and the daylight less. It is not properly light until after prime now, and we say vespers by artificial light already.

The small allowance of Christmas cards which the monk is allowed to send out—only twelve personal ones—have been delivered to our cells already. I shall never get used to this ration, however long I am in the monastery. I receive many times that number. I hope people understand. I try to overcome this by sending one card to cover a group of people where possible. All these are a sure sign that winter is rapidly overtaking us.

The gardening squad are on duty preparing the garden for the winter and the farming squad are busy ploughing the fields. If they both can get finished before the hard frosts come, these will break up the soil for them far better than it can be done by the hand of man. I watched the ploughs going up and down, the garden rotor plough making hard work of it and the multiple plough behind the tractor in the fields, changing the surface of ragged vegetation and grass into neat chocolate-coloured rows of furrows, like pleats in velvet cloth. All kinds of birds follow the plough, picking up the feast of grubs turned up by it.

Bonfire Night was celebrated a week or two ago. We do not hear much of it out here in the country but there was a sound like small-arms fire yesterday. I thought it was fireworks, but I hear today, that it was an invasion from Mars! The B.B.C. television unit were making a film on land near the monastery—hence the small-arms fire. I

wonder when it will be screened? If our experience of
television is anything to go by, probably never.

We do not often have the chance to see television, only
when something of national interest is screened such as a
coronation or other major state occasion. However, when
anything happens like this, locally, one's interest is
aroused.

Winter
Sunday lunchtime. The midday meal being over and not
having any duty allocated to me, it was a good opportunity
to take a brisk walk through the woods in the wintry
sunshine. The trees are bare now, the fallen leaves form-
ing a springy carpet to walk on. The cemetery clearing
looks very forlorn. It is kept clear of leaves and weeds by
the monks on garden duty. The grass is also kept close
mown in the growing season, but now they are fighting a
losing battle against the falling leaves. There they lie, the
departed members of the community, in their order of
precedence as they were in life, with the line of departed
abbots in the front row, facing their flock. The last to be
buried has not had a cross erected yet and will not, until
the ground subsides. The wood has been ordered and delivered to the workshop for the cross to be made and the
inscription carved upon it. Opepe wood is used, since it is
hard and virtually never rots.

I well remember the abbot's passing. A venerable monk
whom some thought to be over-severe. He was a kindly
man though, in spite of his gruff exterior. He had been a
regular Naval Officer before he was professed as a monk,
so that probably accounted for his severity. Anyway, he
knew how to handle men. There was a bunch of flowers on
the grave, probably from our greenhouses where the
sanctuary flowers are cultivated. A pity to see them wilt in
the cold.

There, lie two monks whom I knew well. A lay brother at
the back there, in front of an intern oblate. Over there lies
a bishop oblate, who had requested a monastic burial, to
which he was entitled.

It is interesting to note that religious orders who move

their location (which is only very rarely) invariably have their dead exhumed and re-buried in the new cemetery.

Standing looking at the graves, brought to the mind the words of Thomas à Kempis, in his *Imitation of Christ*. After a long dissertation, he finishes with, "Be ready at all times, and so live that death may never find you unprepared". I strongly recommend this book.

I had stood still whilst all the memories flooded back and I was brought back to reality by a shiver, as the cold found my bones.

The first thick fog of the year. We are not overtroubled by fog here in the open country, although when we do have it, it is usually a bad one.

The main centre of fog seems to have been in the North. The M1 was badly affected and there were many accidents. The trouble again is human failure. I have noticed that when I slow for bad weather conditions, in the monastery car, other vehicles flash past me at speed—the well known 'motorway madness'.

We have been adopted by a bantam cock. He is a fine specimen with his bright red comb and flowing tail feathers. The first day, we spotted him on our lawn and he was not averse to being hand fed. He inspected the chicken runs disdainfully and made no attempt to enter. Probably he realized that our cockerel was bigger than he.

He was missing at night but re-appeared the next day. We found he was sleeping in a holly tree. He would fly up to the bottom branches, then scramble up and go to sleep with his head under his wing.

Enquiries were made of the surrounding farms to locate the owner, without avail, until we located his farm, further away than we expected. The only reason we could think of for his having travelled such a long way, was that he had left home because his harem nagged him. We rounded him up. This involved about a dozen monks, a lot of "chuck chucking" and several handfuls of corn. We returned him to his owner. The next morning he was back on our lawn again. He evidently preferred the monastic life to the married state. This time, he was caught and taken home for good.

It is now freezing really hard. The night sky is clear and the stars stand out like diamonds on a black velvet pad. Some of them appear to be coloured but I suppose this is an optical illusion. Everything is deadly quiet so that all sounds carry with startling clarity. I could hear a car a long way off. Someone coughed far away along the lane. A dog barked on a nearby farm.

The grass glistens like a silver carpet. The trees stand out starkly, stripped of their leaves. The shrubs look as if they have been covered with dust sheets. Suddenly, feeling the cold, I went indoors.

Mid Advent. Gaudete Sunday. As usual, out come the bright pink vestments, only used on this day. One of the monks says they are "shocking pink", after the colour of a lady's nail varnish, or so he says. I wonder how he knows?

Just after dawn this morning, the sky, looking out to the east, presented a picture of incredible beauty.

There was a red glow shining behind the bare trees of our woods, with the stark outline of the trees standing out behind it in black. Above the trees, the sky was pale blue, with irregular bars of fluffy pink clouds running across it—an intense pastel pink shade. If painted by an artist, one would say it was overdone.

30th January. Very cold with snow and freezing fog, and to cap it all, no central heating. This is thanks to the oil tanker drivers' strike. One finds it difficult to cultivate charitable thoughts towards them under these circumstances.

The few electric fires in the monastery have been gathered in for the use of the sick. The rest of us put on extra woollies and our cloaks, and shiver. I wonder what will happen to the sick if the electricity men strike as well? I suppose we could keep them going if we brought them all down to the senior common-room and lit a log fire, as we do at Christmas? There would then be no shortage of volunteers for sick visiting.

The Feast of the Purification comes round. Or should I call it the Feast of the Presentation, according to our 'reformers'? Apparently it is old-fashioned to give too much honour to Mary the mother of Our Lord.

The Saturday office, which used to be dedicated to Our Lady, has been altered and demoted to a mere commemoration at lauds. I rejoice to see that the Mass is still the *Salva Sancta Parens* however. The old Candlemass was really a festival of light. When I participated in it when I first entered the monastery, I was profoundly moved. Today, the candles are only used for the procession into chapel and are then extinguished. They are not even re-lit for the reading of the gospel.

However, I suppose that one must be thankful that reformation is always followed by counter-reformation. Things may get better.

Shrove Tuesday. The winter still hangs on, but the end is at last in sight. This is the last day before Lent when the fats and oils were used up in preparation for the Lenten Fast.

We are completing our preparations for Lent. Our books for Lenten reading have been handed out. This is the last day that we shall meet in the common-room for recreation until the end of Lent. Instead we do our Lenten reading in our cells.

Each one of us has drawn up our Lenten Rule and submitted it to the abbot. This special list of Lenten penance and self-denial must neither be too strict that it might damage health, nor too slack. One has to keep to the middle path to get it passed by the abbot.

Tomorrow is Ash Wednesday, with its special ceremonies. Our Lenten fast then commences. One hopes that the long winter will have given way to warmer weather by the time that Easter arrives.

Having finished my story, I trust that in some small way, I

191

have been instrumental in dispelling the illusions that some people have, regarding the religious life. I hope that I have convinced people that monks and nuns are very ordinary people, with strong religious convictions. Their way of life is not suited to all but it is not as strange as most people imagine. There is a lot of fun and jollity within the monastery, and, contrary to popular belief, monks are very happy people.